CAFES

AND

CABARETS

OF

MONTMARTRE

—

MARIEL OBERTHUR

—

P

Gibbs M. Smith, Inc.
Peregrine Smith Books
Salt Lake City
1984

English Translation by Sheila Azoulai

First edition, 1984

Copyright © 1984 by Gibbs M. Smith, Inc.

This is a Peregrine Smith Book,
published by Gibbs M. Smith, Inc.,
P.O. Box 667,
Layton, UT 84041

Designed by M. Clane Graves

Manufactured in the United States of America

Library of Congress Cataloging in Publication Data
Oberthur, Mariel, 1945-
      Cafes and cabarets of Montmartre.
      "Peregrine Smith books."
      Bibliography: p. 93
      1. Arts, French—France—Paris. 2. Paris (France)—
Nightclubs, dance halls, etc.—History. 3. Montmartre
(Paris, France)—Nightclubs, dance halls, etc.—History.
4. Artists—France—Paris—Social conditions. I. Title.
NX549.P2024 1984   700'.944'361   83-27104

Photographs from museums in France
courtesy of the Réunion des Musées Nationaux—Paris.

DEDICATED TO MONSIEUR JEAN ADHEMAR

CONTENTS

Jean Beraut, *Femme
au café*, oil, ca. 1890.
Musée des Arts
Décoratifs, Paris.

MONTMARTRE

Montmartre, after the war of 1870 and the Commune of Paris, was in the midst of great transformation during the early days of the Third Republic. Urban development had been underway in Montmartre since the destruction of the unpopular toll-gates and wall surrounding Paris under the Second Empire. This evolution dated back to 1830 when many townhouses were built around Notre-Dame de Lorette, the Martyrs's barricade and the place Blanche to house writers, artists and the *grands bourgeois*.

In 1860 the Butte Montmartre was incorporated into the City of Paris. Before then, Montmartre had been an outlying suburb, where no prudent traveler would venture at certain times of the day. Now, towards the close of the nineteenth century, it was an area much sought out, not only for its pleasant atmosphere but also for its rural character

Montmartre was soon to acquire a reputation as a place for entertainment, "pleasure" and festivity, a reputation that would last for many years. Famous throughout the world, Montmartre was a symbol of gaiety and Bohemian life, bursting with artistic and literary activity; it soon became the capital of the arts and one of the intellectual centers of Paris. In the years between 1870 and 1900, the area around the Nouvelle Athènes, place Pigalle, boulevard Rochechouart and the Batignolles became an important focal point for intellectual life in Paris, even surpassing the influence of the Latin Quarter.

A close study of life in the cafés, cabarets and balls is essential not only to understand the social development of Montmartre, but also to grasp the true nature of the world in which the artists lived. The café, cabaret and popular ball, intrinsically French institutions, catered to all different tastes. The number of political, artistic and literary cafés in Montmartre kept increasing. In a series of articles published in the *Courrier Français* in 1886, Emmanuel Patrick described all the cafés in Paris, district by district, one by one, noting the distinctive features of each. The district of Montmartre was most certainly included.

Unlike the very fashionable Salon, the only recognized social institution of the seventeenth and eighteenth centuries, the café, brasserie and popular ball were open to all. Neither invitation nor introduction was necessary. Everyone was freely admitted, no restraints and no obligations imposed. To these cafés the habitués would come, seeking to share pleasure and amusement.

Léon Daudet, faithful habitué of the cafés around place Pigalle wrote: *"Le café était l'école de la franchise et de la drôlerie spontanée, tandis que le Salon sauf chez Madame de Loynes ou une Foemina, est en général l'école des poncifs et de la mode imbécile. Le café a donné l'exquis Verlaine, et le grand et pur Moréas, le Salon, Robert de Montesquiou et je ne sais combien de muses inutiles ou comiques."*[1]

(The café was a school where sincerity and humor reigned, whereas the Salon, with the exception of Madame de Loynes's or a certain Foemina's, was usually more frivolous and affectatious. The café gave us the exquisite Verlaine, the great Moréas, the Salon, Robert de Montesquiou and how many other incompetent or comical muses I don't know.)

In *Salons et Journaux* Daudet also wrote of Courteline, a loyal Auberge du Clou habitué: *"Mon père qui le chérissait et savait par coeur Le Train de 8 H.47, me disait souvent: Comment attirer Courteline? Les Salons l'embêtent. Il faudrait lui aménager ici un petit café avec de la sciure et des boules de métal où mettre des torchons. Attention, ripostait Coppée: J'ai connu une jeune femme qui avait organisé cela chez elle, afin de retenir son mari. Mais il déserta bientôt le café conjugal, sous prétexte que la bière manquait de pression."*

(My father, who knew by heart and cherished *Le Train de 8 H.47*, used to say to me: How can we entice Courteline? The salons bore him. We shall have to fix up a little café, complete with sawdust and metal dishtowel knobs for him. Be careful, retorted Coppée: I once knew a young woman who, in order to keep a hold on her husband did that very same thing in her home. However, before long her husband abandoned the conjugal café, where he found the beer too flat for his taste.)[2]

Although they failed to realize the magnitude of social and intellectual influence cafés were to have, the Goncourts had already foreseen by 1856 a brilliant career ahead for cafés and cabarets. For the Goncourts, cafés and cabarets at that time were simply places of pleasure: *"Le café me semble une distraction bien en enfance. Il me semble qu'on trouvera plus ou mieux. Il y aura des endroits, où avec un gaz, un je ne sais quoi, on vous emplira de gaîté comme d'une bière; des philtres qui vous gratteront la rate; des garçons qui vous verseront par tout le corps et tout l'esprit une sorte de paix et de joie; du paradis à la tasse, de véritables débits de consolation, où les pensées feront peau neuve et peau belle, où l'on retrouvera le cours de l'âme pour une heure."*[3]

(It appears to me that café entertainment is just emerging. In the years ahead there will be more and better entertainment, where a sparkling drink, or I know not what, will fill you like a beer with delight; love filters will soothe your spleen; waiters will pour serenity and joy into body and mind, paradise in a glass; a true source of comfort where thoughts will give birth to a new and beautiful life, and where your soul will be discovered anew for an hour or two.)

Edmond de Goncourt seems to have forgotten the artistic and literary cafés and cabarets where *l'esprit montmartrois* was born. For Goncourt, the café was a place where one sipped absinthe and quaffed tankards of beer while enjoying the company of "loose women," or they were dens of corruption described as such by Balzac and Zola.

The artistic café and cabaret of Montmartre first saw the light of day under the Second Empire. In *Raphael et Gambrinus*, John Grand-Carteret quotes the text of a booklet, *Les Dames*, published in 1860, where there is a description of the origins of the Montmartre cafés:

"A son origine, c'était un cercle familier de jeunes gens qui se

réunissaient pour causer librement politique et littérature. Le Maître de l'établissement, qui prenait part lui aussi aux réunions et quelquefois les présidait, ne cherchait pas fortune. Il se contentait d'une clientèle peu nombreuse à laquelle il fournissait pour un prix modique, un local simple et de bonnes consommations. C'était au beau temps de la bohème: de cette bohème dont Murger a raconté l'histoire. . . . De futurs hommes de lettres, des peintres, des sculpteurs, quelques étudiants, composaient ces réunions dont on peut chercher dans le café Momus une lointaine image. Les murs des anciens caboulots sont ornés de dessins originaux, quelques uns sont dus aux crayons d'hommes qui ont aujourd'hui un nom distingué comme on peut le voir au café Genin, rue Vavin et au caboulot de la rue des Cordiers.[4]

(In the beginning the café was a place where young people could meet, mix freely, speak openly of politics and literature. Often the proprietor of the establishment participated in these informal meetings, sometimes even presiding, not particularly concerned about making money. He was happy to provide his small clientele with an ordinary room and good drinks at a low price. These were the good old days of Bohemia and the Bohemian life described by Murger. . . . These social gatherings brought together future men of letters, painters, sculptors and students, a scene which brings to mind the café Momus. Some of the original crayon sketches by artists considered famous and distinguished today still hang on the walls of old cafés such as the café Genin on rue Vavin and the café on rue des Cordiers.)

Thus was born the cabaret and the artistic and literary café. An ever-increasing number were to line the streets of Paris especially in Montmartre, future homes of painters, sculptors, musicians, poets, critics and an assortment of clamorous youths, thirsting for poetry and art. The center of Paris and the *beaux quartiers* were left behind by a number of artists who set up their ateliers in this new neighborhood.

Degas first resided on rue Blanche, then rue Frochot near his friend

MONTMARTRE

Daniel Halévy who was on rue Douai. From 1865 to 1867 Manet lived on boulevard des Batignolles, then from 1876 to 1878 on rue de Saint-Pétersbourg and finally on rue d'Amsterdam.

Renoir's studio was to be found at 35 rue Saint-Georges. In 1875 Forain moved in at the corner of the rue de Tourlaque and rue Lepic, Willette resided on rue Véron, Toulouse-Lautrec on rue de Tourlaque, Steinlen on rue Caulaincourt. On his arrival in Paris, Picasso lived on rue Gabrielle, and his Catalan friends, Santiago Rusinol and Ramon Casas, at the Moulin de la Galette. Suzanne Valadon and Miguel Utrillo both lived on rue Cortot. These are only a few examples among many.

Long before Montparnasse, Montmartre became a sought-out haven for artists and their ateliers.

After the Revolution, the role of the *patron* in the studio disappeared. The atelier no longer was the place of refuge it formerly had been, except perhaps at Cormon's. The artist found himself cut off from the outside world. When nightfall would come, the lack of light would force work to be abandoned until the following day. For these reasons and an urgent desire to communicate, to converse, artists found an ideal sanctuary in cafés and popular balls.[5]

The ambiance of café life began to evolve, and the artists who gathered there influenced one another in both their manner of painting and expression. From 1875 on, the café, cabaret and café-concert became central themes in "modernist painting," an aesthetic propounded by the Impressionist painters who worked beside Manet and Degas. Except in works by a very few Flemish artists, these were new themes for painters. Be it Manet, Degas, Forain, Van Gogh, Lautrec or Picasso, they all treated the café subject differently.

Manet was interested in the psychology of the café people he depicted. He painted them around a table, a glass of beer at hand, usually in cafés where women most often did the serving, a startling innovation in 1875. As we shall see, beer occupies a very prominent

MONTMARTRE

place in the works of Manet.

Degas was fascinated with the play of light on objects and people in the cafés. The design and paintings in the cafés and café-concerts allowed Degas to express his obvious pleasure in the ambiance within, and let him study the effects of light on people's faces, bodies and shadows. Soon, electric lighting made the public places more brightly lit and Degas was keenly interested in the way it distorted the objects around him, creating new visions.

Where Degas was intrigued by the effects of light, Forain preferred descriptive painting. His paintings take on a documentary nature.

Cafés and café society are also recurring themes in Van Gogh's paintings. His expression of the café life is highly emotional. In his two works, *Une Italienne* (Musée du Louvre, Paris) and *La femme au Tambourin* (Rijksmuseum, Amsterdam) he paints the woman he loves, the proprietress of the café du Tambourin on boulevard de Clichy. In his other paintings depicting cafés such as *L'Absinthe* (Rijksmuseum, Amsterdam), *Restaurant à Arles* (Mrs. M. S. Danforth Collection, Providence), *Intérieur de Restaurant à Paris* (Rijksmuseum Khöller Muller, Otterlo), the cafés are all empty. Atmosphere is created through shadows. In this way, Van Gogh expressed his loneliness, anguish, and fear of death.

In contrast, Toulouse-Lautrec's paintings are studies of society at that time. The café and cabaret are his favorite subjects and like Degas, Lautrec was interested in the play of light on faces, allowing him to go beyond mere description and investigate the depths of the soul. In *Au Rat Mort*, Lucy Jourdain Cabinet particulier 7 (Courtauld Institute, London), Lautrec endeavours to reproduce the atmosphere of the "private room" in cafés. In his portraits of Van Gogh (Rijksmuseum, Amsterdam) and Suzanne Valadon, *La gueule de bois* (Fogg Art Museum, Boston), Lautrec captures their dreamlike expression induced by the café atmosphere, without representing decor. In all his other works depicting the Moulin de la Galette, the Elysée-Montmartre or the Moulin Rouge, Toulouse-Lautrec recreates their gay atmosphere and cheerful tone. What lends great interest and conveys all the more realism and life to these studies in manners is the fact that all the people can be named: La Goulue, Nini Patte en l'Air, Grille d'Egout, Albert Tinchant, Yvette Guilbert. . . .

Steinlen, too, painted many café scenes. Of particular interest to him was the portrayal of different social classes such as laundresses, dressmakers and all the various Montmartre characters downing *"un petit verre au zinc."* These paintings can be considered as complements to the Montmartre-based novels written during the same period, from Zola to Paul Alexis.

It is also of interest to note the development in the decor of the cafés and cabarets of Montmartre. The artistic cafés had their own particular style; paintings and drawings by café habitués decorated the walls. Gradually this trend made its way into the cabaret. Gilded walls and painted ceilings were not, however, a common sight in the Montmartre cafés, except for a few such as the café Guerbois on avenue de Clichy, and the Nouvelle Athènes on place Pigalle.

The others had their own individual style. Here began a fashion that was to become very widespread indeed. An article in *Le Monde,* September 22, 1885 read: *"Au cabaret, au café classique, aux immenses glaces, aux salons aux filets dorés, aux chaises Empire, aux vastes billards et aux canapés revêtus de velours écarlates, ont succédé des salles sombres, éclairées par des vitraux artistiques."* And in *Paris Carnaval,* October 30, 1885: *"Heureuse idée de remplacer le plafond blanc par quelque chose de pittoresque et faire varier la monotonie du tablier blanc et de la veste noire par des 'fracs.'"*

(The great golden mirrors, Empire chairs, the scarlet velvet sofas, immense billiard halls, and gilt-adorned drawing rooms of the café and cabaret have given way to more somber cafés where light is diffused through stained glass windows. [And in *Paris Carnaval*:] What a wonderful idea it was to replace the traditional white ceiling with something more picturesque and to vary the dull white apron or black jacket with something more interesting, like 'tailcoats'.)

The days of dinners and suppers served upon white linen were over. From then on tableclothes were no longer used or, if at all, only the checkered type. To compete for business with the café next door, every proprietor came up with a distinct style to attract a larger clientele.

In Montmartre, around the fashionable district of the Nouvelle Athènes, the Grande Pinte was the first café where paintings and other objects were displayed on the walls, recalling and imitating taverns built during the reign of Henry IV in the seventeenth century. The proprietor would ask each artist to produce a palette for his café.[6]

The Chat Noir, the Auberge du Clou, the Abbaye de Thélème and the Tambourin would later on do the same. In such a way the café became a showplace where the habitués could exhibit their paintings, sketches, drawings and engravings. In short, the café became an art gallery.

The artistic Salon was no longer the middleman between artist and public, and the considerable rise in the number of painters and illustrators meant that cafés, cabarets, and even popular balls became ideal exhibition places for the artists to show their works. In fact, many artists owed their popularity to these new "galleries." Art galleries were almost non-existent at the time and those that did exist catered only to academic painters; the works of Montmartre artists were not accepted there.

In 1889 Van Gogh exhibited his crepons at the Tambourin; later, along with Lautrec, he exhibited works by his friends: *"Besnard y a vendu son premier tableau, Anquetin a vendu une étude, moi, j'ai fait l'échange avec Gauguin."* (Besnard sold his first painting there, Anquetin sold a study, and Gauguin and I made an exchange.) (*Correspondance de V. V. Gogh,* Vol. 3, letter 510 F.)

The walls at the Chat Noir were permanently covered with paintings by the habitués. Customers could buy them depending on Salis's mood at the time. There was a similar practice at the Auberge du Clou. At the Abbaye de Thélème on place Pigalle, artists could leave their works for a month or two in the hope of selling them.

The decor in cafés and cabarets created by artists from Montmartre such as Willette, Henri Pille, Tanzi and Lautrec (if indeed he did decorate the cellar at the Auberge du Clou) have almost all disappeared. We know of their existence, however, through illustrations published in newspapers of the day. Only the decorations for the Auberge du Clou and for the Chat Noir can still be seen.

Each decor had its own particular theme reflecting social realities of the times and the individual atmosphere of each café and each cabaret. Moreover, the painter revealed to varying degrees his own personality.

At the Rat Mort, the decor, which was quite descriptive, related the edifying life of a rat.

At the Abbaye de Thélème and the Grande Pinte, Henri Pille and Tanzi were clearly inspired by the Middle Ages.

At the Auberge du Clou and the Chat Noir, Willette let his imagination flow freely and became the interpreter of the fantasies flourishing in each of the two establishments. In his paintings, Willette expressed an insatiable desire to profit fully from life with all the underlying dreams it implied. Indeed, behind his outward light-heartedness, Willette transposed profound emotions with truth and perception. The mood expressed in these paintings was never optimistic.

At the Taverne du Bagne, the decor was quite singular: the history of the Communards and their deportation. The same can be said for the decor at the Divan Japonais: *"Tout y est chinois"* (everything there is Chinese).

MONTMARTRE

In each establishment, illustrated menus for the clients accentuated the atmosphere already created by the decor. Willette designed the menus for the Auberge du Clou and for the Nouvelle Athènes, Henri Somm for the Rat Mort and George Auriol for the Chat Noir.

The characters or themes depicted in these menus such as the black cat, Pierrot, the dead rat, and the *"petites femmes"* were the same as those found in the decor. Poor Pierrot is scratched by the cat, the rat ends up dying roasted or swinging from the gallows, Willette's *"petites femmes"* are rather scantily clad. Here again we can appreciate a feature of Montmartre painting and humor.

Another innovation of Montmartre cafés and cabarets was the publication of illustrated humorous newspapers. The popular balls did not, however, circulate their own papers. A law protecting the freedom of the press in 1881 led to a proliferation of illustrated newspapers. And in Montmartre, the satirical press was experiencing great effervescence. There were two types of illustrated papers: those published by publishing houses such as *Le Courrier Français,* and those published by cafés and cabarets such as *Le Chat Noir, L'Auberge du Clou, Le Divan Japonais, La Gazette du Bagne, Le Mirliton.*

The writers for *Le Courrier Français* frequented the Rat Mort and the Abbaye de Thélème, the balls at the Elysée-Montmartre or the Moulin Rouge, producing a wealth of drawings and information about the establishments. *Le Courrier Français* is not, however, representative of the true illustrated café paper.

The best and the most celebrated publication was *Le Chat Noir,* which was also the longest running café newspaper. A closer look at this paper is essential for an understanding of the social and political concerns of the time as well as the preoccupations of those who frequented cabarets.

There were two types of drawings published in *Le Chat Noir, Le Divan Japonais, La Gazette du Bagne* and *Le Mirliton:* social drawings and political drawings with caricatures whose satire was stringently biting.

The years from 1885 to 1900 witnessed the flourishing of caricatures. Gavarni, Daumier, and their contemporaries opened wide the door for an art form which would find its apogée at the very end of the century, an art form whose influence is found in today's comic strips. These caricatures mirrored the aesthetics of the wall decorations executed by Willette, Pille and others.

The caricature became a veritable language, its symbols and images grasped by everyone in an atmosphere of complicity. Not only was the artist's psychology revealed in this art form but also that of the newspaper's reader. The artist could express his fears, his dreams, and his phantasms, transcribe his inner vision of the world and communicate his emotions and preoccupations to others.

When Willette and Steinlen at the Chat Noir chose to illustrate a specific character such as the cat or Pierrot, it seems evident that they were portraying themselves. Other illustrators such as Fau, Uzès, Ferdinandus, Caran d'Ache, and de Sta, on the other hand, exploited comic situations in fashion at the end of the nineteenth century which were also being developed in literature: *qui pro quo* between husband and wife, misfortunes of women, farcical intrigues, stories dealing with Negroes, military life, chauvinism and bourgeois behavior.

Shadow theatre reached its height in the cafés and cabarets around the Butte Montmartre and, in particular, at the Chat Noir. Shadow theatre was a new attraction offered by the cafés. At a time when there was no cinema or television, shadow theatre provided a means of bringing together words, forms and music. The Chat Noir was not the only cabaret to present such a show. The Auberge du Clou and the Rochefoucault imitated the Chat Noir and after 1900, the Boîte à Fursy, the Quat'z'arts and the Lune Rousse did as well.

Behind a cloth screen, a moveable or fixed decor would be positioned and manipulated by *"artistes machinistes."* Placed farther away, a lamp lit up the screen upon which the decor and silhouettes were outlined. In the café itself a *"bonimenteur,"*[7] and at the Chat Noir, Salis himself, would accompany the action with a running commentary. From the wings, musicians or a chorus might be heard.

Shadow theatre remained popular for only a short time, barely twenty years, for it was soon replaced by the advent of moving pictures.

During the World Exhibitions held in Paris from 1867 to 1878, beer became the favorite drink of café, cabaret and ball habitués, replacing absinthe which was to be finally prohibited in 1915. At that time, the price of a glass of beer was modest, about 50 centimes. At the Chat Noir, Salis decided to increase the price of beer and include it in the admission to the shadow theatre. Although frequently practiced in present day cabarets, this custom was not at all popular then.

Widely recognized and appreciated by the public, beer held an important role in the works of the artists. Manet's *L'Amour de l'art* (May 1932) in particular conveys this attention to beer.

It can be said, in fact, that Manet was a true beer enthusiast. Around 1880, a quarrel broke out between the partisans of French beer and German beer. In 1885, Belloc, the engraver Manet painted in *Le Bon Bock* (Philadelphia, Museum of Art), published a humorous paper called *Le Bon Bock* from February 21 to July 18, 1855 where he defended the superiority of French beer over German beer. It was also Belloc, who in 1875, inaugurated the "Bon Bock dinners."[8]

In many of Manet's paintings, a tankard of beer is prominently displayed on a table in the foreground: *Le café* (London, National Gallery); *Les deux bockeuses: deux femmes buvant de la bière* (Glasgow, Burrel Collection); and in *Au café, la brasserie de Reichshoffen* (Winterthur, Fondation Oskar Reinhart).

Manet went even further in his study of beer in cafés. At the time, it was unique for women to serve beer, and in several paintings Manet drew attention to this phenomenon. Neither Degas nor Forain nor

Steinlen sought to portray such social novelties.

Degas was more interested in absinthe. In his painting *L'Absinthe* (Paris, Musée du Louvre, 1878-1879), Degas shows that this drink was still consumed and appreciated in Montmartre cafés. At the same time, George Moore in *Confessions of a Young Englishman* evokes the odor of absinthe in the café Nouvelle Athènes where he was a faithful customer. Absinthe was usually drunk in the late afternoon between five and seven o'clock: *"C'est l'heure verte,"* the time when one would *"étouffe les perroquets."*[9]

The theme of beer, wine, and absinthe drinking was also portrayed in other types of decoration, especially in wall frescos in cafés. Willette's work at the Auberge du Clou is one example; André Gill's painting at the Grand Bock on rue Dancourt, depicting a naked woman balancing two enormous tankards of beer on her breasts is another example. This painting has unfortunately been lost.

Beer, obviously, goes hand in hand with singing, and songs held a place of honor in Montmartre cafés and cabarets. Interpreted by their authors, Mac Nab, Bruant, Meusy, Jules Jouy or by professional singers, Montmartre songs are neither bawdy nor affected. They are full of humor and imagination, of *l'esprit montmartrois*, reflecting popular preoccupations as did the paintings of the day. They are realistic songs akin to Zola's novels.

The poet-chansonnier par excellence was Aristide Bruant who, with *A la Bastille, A Menilmontant, A Saint-Lazare, A la Glacière*, or *Les Petit's Joyeux*, introduced cabaret songs into café-concerts. Wanting to give the impression of having frequented low company, the public, who returned again and again to Montmartre, could be often heard humming café and cabaret songs in the streets of Paris.

The years between 1885 and 1900 witnessed the great success of the poet-chansonnier. Numerous, whether well known or not, they appeared in cabarets every evening, each with his own repertory and public: Xavier Privas, Fursy, Pierre Trimouillat, Jehan Rictus, Vincent Hyspa, Dominique Bonnaud, Mac Nab, Charles Cros, Victor Meusy, Gaston Couté, and others.

It is perhaps the *Hareng Saur* by Charles Cros that the cabaret public in Montmartre preferred, interpreted by its author or by the younger Coquelin or Galipaux. Everyone knew it by heart and eagerly anticipated every line:

Il était un grand mur blanc—nu, nu, nu,
Contre ce mur une échelle—haute, haute, haute,
Et par terre, un hareng saur—sec, sec, sec.

(It was a big white wall—naked, naked, naked,
Against the wall a ladder—high, high, high,
And on the ground, a red herring—dry, dry, dry.)

At the end of the nineteenth century the history of Montmartre merged with that of the cafés, cabarets and balls so popular with the public. These establishments bore true witness to life in Montmartre. The cafés and cabarets welcomed the people who came just for amusement and entertainment, Impressionists defined their doctrines while humorists and fanciful writers created *l'esprit montmartrois*. This colorful blend made Montmartre a center of art and literature, the preferred *quartier* for certain bohemians and noisy youth who were full of life and yet never far from everyday reality.

MONTMARTRE

Montmartre, sans artistes
Futuristes
Réalistes
Ou Cubistes
Et sans ses nombreux "fumistes"
Exerçant tous les métiers,
Ne serait qu'un des plus tristes quartiers.
(anonyme)

(Montmartre, without artists
Futurists
Realists
Or Cubists
And without its many "jokers"
Practicing every kind of trade,
Would be but a very dull place.)
(anonymous)

Edgar Degas,
L'Absinthe, oil,
1878-1879. Musée du
Louvre, Paris. In the
same decor painted by
Forain, Degas
portrayed Marcellin
Desboutin seated next
to the actress Ellen
André. They were
both frequent
customers at the
Nouvelle Athènes.

Left: Edouard Manet,
La Prune, oil, 1878.
National Gallery,
Washington, D.C.
Collection of Mr. and
Mrs. Paul Mellon,
1971. The young
woman seated at a
café table, a glass of
plum brandy in front
of her, and an unlit
cigarette in her hand
might be one of
Manet's models who
frequented the Rat
Mort. If so, the café
depicted would not be
the Nouvelle Athènes,
as has been often
suggested.

Above: Jean Louis
Forain, *Intérieur de la
Nouvelle Athènes*, color
drawing, 1878.
Cabinet des Dessins,
Musée du Louvre,
Paris. This is the only
drawing representing
in detail the decor
and atmosphere of the
Nouvelle Athènes.

27

Above: Edouard
Manet, *Au café*, oil,
1878. Oskar Reinhart
Foundation,
Winterthur. This
painting, also known
as *Un coin de café*,
depicts Henri Guérard
and Ellen André at
the Nouvelle Athènes
and not, as others
have suggested, at
another café. Several
details in the painting
recall the Nouvelle
Athènes: the small pot
for matches on the
table, the form of the
chairs, and the curtain
pattern.

Right: Van Gogh,
L'Italienne, oil, 1887.
Musée du Louvre,
Paris. Still very much
in love with La
Segatori, Van Gogh
painted her portrait
before the summer of
1887. Even though
Van Gogh and La
Segatori had had an
argument, Van Gogh
wrote his brother

Théo: "I still have
feelings for her and I
hope she still has
some for me." Van
Gogh painted her
seated on a chair
dressed in regional
Italian costume.

28

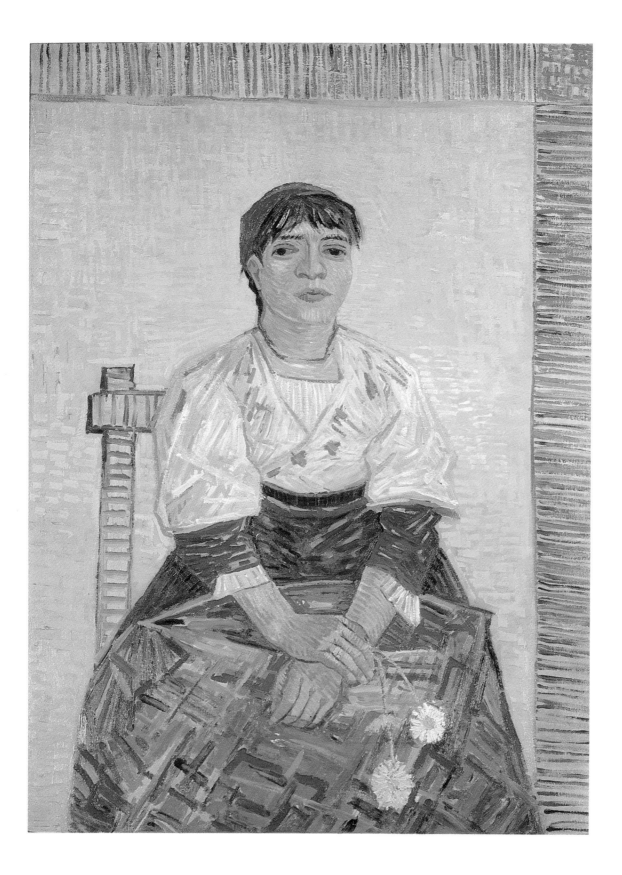

Left: Edouard Manet, *Le café*, oil, 1878. The Burrel Collection, Glasgow Museums & Art Galleries. In this sketch, Manet portrayed a barmaid, iconographically a new subject and one that he was to use frequently. It is difficult to determine if this scene takes place in the Nouvelle Athènes.

Above: Edgar Degas, *Femmes à la terrasse d'un café*, pastel, 1877. Cabinet des Dessins, Musée du Louvre, Paris. These young women seated at a café curiously resemble those painted by Manet. The background depicts the place Pigalle which means that this café would, most likely, be the Rat Mort.

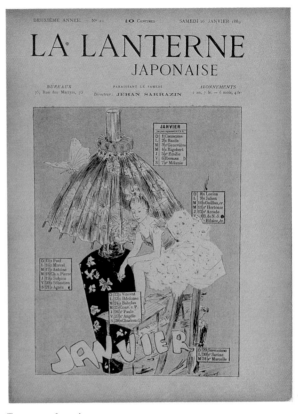

Two covers from the
*Journal du Divan
Japonais*. Musée de
Montmartre, Paris.

THE
CAFES

LE GUERBOIS

lready before the War of 1870 and the Commune of Paris, Manet and his friends gathered at the café Guerbois (9 grande rue des Batignolles, today avenue de Clichy—not far from the place de Clichy). Tiring of the café de Bade and the Tortoni on the *grands boulevards*, they had sought out cafés nearer their ateliers in the vicinity of the Batignolles. With his work *Déjeuner sur l'herbe* (1863, Musée du Louvre, Paris), Manet emerged as the leader of the new generation:

"Ils étaient une douzaine. . . . A. Legros, Whistler, Fantin-Latour, s'étaient joints des écrivains, Babou, Vignaux, Duranty, Zola; un graveur: Belloc immortalisé depuis par Le Bon Bock; un autre graveur: Desboutin qui fut aussi un peintre et un modèle et qui s'est fait une large place parmi ses contemporains non comme modèle mais comme peintre et comme graveur; un paysagiste délicat: Guillemet; un orientaliste, Tobar; un universaliste: Zacharie Astruc qui emploie avec une égale passion le pinceau, la massette et la plume. . . . A la longue des noms nouveaux s'ajouteront: Degas, Renoir, Monet, Pissarro."[10]

(There were about twelve of them. . . . A. Legros, Whistler, Fantin-Latour would be joined by the writers Babou, Gignaux, Duranty, Zola; the engraver Belloc who was to be immortalized in Manet's *Le Bon Bock*; another engraver, Desboutin, who was equally well known at the time as a painter though less so as an artist's model; a painter, Guillemet; an orientalist, Tobar; a universalist, Zacharie Astruc, who wielded the paintbrush, the chisel and the pen with

equal passion. . . . And, finally, the later arrivals: Degas, Renoir, Monet, Pissarro.)

The Guerbois was depicted by few artists, and only Manet did paintings of its interior. Furthermore, we have no idea of the café's façade as there are no postcards depicting the Guerbois. [11]

Several writers, however, wrote about the Guerbois. Armand Sylvestre [12] was one and, in particular, Duranty, who in one of his short stories, "La double vie de Louis Seguin," wrote:

"La première salle blanche et dorée pleine de glaces, criblée de lumière, ressemble à la terrasse d'un café de boulevard. Mais dès qu'on est entré dans la seconde salle, l'endroit devient étonnant, on se trouve dans une vaste crypte à plafond bas."[13]

(The first room, all white and gold, riddled with lights and full of mirrors, looks like the terrace of any café on the boulevards. But upon entering the second room, the place becomes astonishing as you find yourself in a huge crypt with a low ceiling.)

Zola focused on the atmosphere at the Guerbois in *L'Oeuvre*, renaming it the café Baudequin:

"Le café Baudequin était situé sur le boulevard des Batignolles, à l'angle de la rue Darcet. Sans que l'on sut pourquoi, la bande l'avait choisi comme lieu de réunion bien que Gagnière seul habitât le quartier. Elle s'y réunissait régulièrement le dimanche soir, puis le jeudi vers 5 heures, ceux qui étaient libres avaient l'habitude d'y paraître un instant."[14]

(The café Baudequin was located on boulevard des Batignolles, at the corner of rue Darcet. Without anyone really knowing

LE GUERBOIS

Michel Lévy, *Portrait de Guerbois*, oil. Musée du Louvre, Paris. Guerbois was the proprietor of the café when the Impressionists were regular customers there. As early as 1889, a successor had already taken over.

LE GUERBOIS

LE GUERBOIS

Edouard Manet. *Intérieur de café*, pencil and blue ink on brown paper, 1869. W. 502. Fogg Art Museum, Boston. This drawing depicts the café Guerbois. The work resembles the café Babois described by Duranty in his short story, "La double vie de Louis Seguin," also dated 1869 and unpublished until Mario Petrone printed it in the *Gazette des Beaux Arts* in 1976.

why, the group had chosen it as their meeting place even though only Gagnière lived in the area. They regularly met there on Sunday evening, and then began meeting also on Thursday around five o'clock. Those who were not busy were in the habit of stopping in for awhile.)

The meetings at the Guerbois probably took place between 1866 (according to John Rewald) and 1875. It was during this period that the "modernist" painters elaborated the Impressionist theory and prepared the first Impressionist exhibition to be held in 1874 at Nadar's on boulevard des Capucines.

"Où est le beau? Tel est le problème; et les débats s'engageaient, ardents, enflammés, entre les chercheurs qu'une même pensée animait et soutenait."[15]

(Where is beauty? That is the problem. And the discussions raged, impassioned, heated, among those seeking an answer, inflamed and sustained by a common pursuit.)

The Guerbois, a café in the style of the Second Empire, was to be abandoned for the Nouvelle Athènes on place Pigalle. The artists gathered at the Guerbois less frequently. Desboutin found the Guerbois too noisy. Renoir and Degas preferred the cafés near Pigalle. This was the end of the Guerbois. Nevertheless, its importance in the history of Impressionist painting is evident.

LA NOUVELLE ATHÈNES

The Nouvelle Athènes was situated on the corner of rue Frochot and rue Pigalle. There was nothing original about its white façade. The terrace on the corner accommodated clients who, making themselves comfortable, would sit and watch the spectacle in the street.

The interior was decorated with paintings by a Montmartre artist, Petit,[16] but there is unfortunately no trace of them. Desboutin, Degas, Forain and Manet portrayed the Nouvelle Athènes in several of their works.

The testimony of George Moore, a young Irishman who came to Paris to study painting at Cabanel's, is quite valuable. He spent more time in the café than at the atelier and was a loyal and regular member at the meetings held there. In *Confessions of a Young Englishman*, George Moore provides a valuable description of the café:

"A partition rising a few feet or more over hats separates the glass front from the

Right: Edouard Manet, *George Moore*, oil, 1879. Metropolitan Museum of Art, New York. Gift of Mrs. Ralph J. Hines, 1955. About this painting, Théodore Duret said: "When Manet had George Moore pose for this portrait, Moore was at the time lost in a sort of aesthetical refinement and rarefied sentimentalism which gives him a vacant, far-away look. Manet seized upon and, as was his habit, even accentuated this physiogonomic feature which is characteristic of Moore's appearance."

Left: Jean Louis Forain, *Le café de la Nouvelle Athènes*, etching, 1878. Bibliothèque Nationale, Paris. At the Nouvelle Athènes, Forain sought out his Impressionist friends and later, Willette, and other Montmartrois dwellers.

LA NOUVELLE ATHÈNES

main body of the café. The usual marble tables are there, and it is there we sat and aestheticised till two o'clock in the morning." [17]

George Moore also evokes the atmosphere in the café by describing its particular early morning smells:

"In the morning, eggs frizzling in butter, the pungent cigarette, coffee and bad cognac; at five o'clock the vegetable smell of absinthe; after the steaming soup ascends from the kitchen and as the evening advances, the mingled smells of cigarettes, coffee and weak beer." [18]

George Moore attended all the meetings at the Nouvelle Athènes: "I went there often and profited greatly from the conversations in which I took part. I was thus able to return to England imbued with a theory of aesthetics." [19]

As at the Guerbois, the exuberance and brilliance displayed in these discussions resulted from a feeling of complicity among the artists and writers,

G. C. A., PARIS

794 Montmartre. — La rue Pigalle — Nouvelle Athènes.

40

created by a deep scorn for official art, and by their desire for renown themselves:

"L'autre fois, grande discussion à propos d'un congrès artistique qu'on annonce. Manet déclarait vouloir y aller, prendre la parole et tomber l'Ecole des Beaux-Arts. Pissarro qui écoutait cela était vaguement inquiet; Duranty, en sage nestor, le rappelait aux moyens pratiques."[20]

(The other day, there was a big discussion about a congress on the arts that had been announced. Manet said he wanted to go there, get up and make a speech and overthrow the Ecole des Beaux-Arts. Pissarro, who was listening, was vaguely worried; Duranty, like a wise nestor, brought him back down to earth.)

Degas also joined in these discussions. But his famous and often quoted words did not please everyone, especially the Goncourts who didn't hold him in their esteem:

"Ce Degas, ce peintre fatiguant avec ses grimaces et ses mots fins du café de la

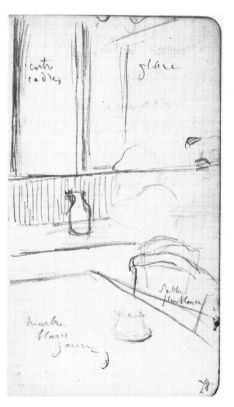

Left: Postcard, the front of the Nouvelle Athènes on the corner of rue Pigalle and rue Frochot.

Center and right: Edgar Degas, two rough sketches for *L'Absinthe*, from Degas's Sketchbook. Print Room, Bibliothèque Nationale, Paris. One of the drawings in the Sketchbook confirms that Ellen André and the engraver Desboutin are the two portrayed in the final *L'Absinthe*.

Nouvelle Athènes."[21] (This Degas at the café Nouvelle Athènes, this tiresome painter with his grimaces and wit.)

In fact, as remembered by Daniel Halévy, the discussions were quite energetic:

"C'était avec Manet et Moore à la Nouvelle Athènes. Nous discutions à n'en plus finir."[22] (It was with Manet and Moore at the Nouvelle Athènes. Our discussions would run on endlessly.)

Between 1878 and 1880, the group of "modernists" around Manet and Degas had become larger at the Nouvelle Athènes.[23] Now there was also Forain, Zandomeneghi, Guèrard, Desboutin . . .[24] and the critics Philippe Burty,[25] Jean Richepin, Paul Alexis, Villiers de l'Isle Adam, Stéphane Mallarmé.[26]

Towards 1880, the clientele at the Nouvelle Athènes changed. No longer needing to get together, the modernist painters were replaced by Willette and his artist friends from Montmartre. In *Feu Pierrot*, Willette depicts the lively atmosphere which flourished even in the morning hours at the Nouvelle Athènes:

"A l'heure de l'apéritif, à onze heures, le café connait une certaine animation; on y rencontre les artistes, les écrivains, les journaleux du pays montmartrois: Gueldry, le peintre de la Grenouillière et des canotiers; l'aquafortiste Henri Somm, causeur délicieux; Achille Melandri, photographe et romancier; le beau Michel de l'Hay; le déjà fameux Mermeix, Henri Pille, la Comtesse Popo; Hoschédé qui s'était ruiné, disait-on plaisamment, à faire chauffer des trains spéciaux pour promener son ami trop admiré le peintre Gérôme; Jean-Louis Forain qui ne pensait qu'à

rivaliser Grévin!; le paysagiste Véron; le peintre Merwarst qui devait disparaître dans l'irruption du Mont Pelé; l'insupportable Tanzi, le peintre biterois des mares et des étangs, enguelant d'une voix enrouée Pierre, Paul, Jacques; le miniaturiste Defeuille; le joyeux moderniste Goeneutte, les peintres Tholer, Faverot, les portraitistes Paul Quinsac, Antonio de la Gandara, tous deux mes anciens camarades d'école; le vieux peintre Bénédict Masson. . . . Il faut compter aussi Bénassit, peintre militaire et illustrateur dont les mots prononcés avec un comique accent britannique, étaient colportés comme ceux de Forain et Aurélien Scholl. . . . "[27]

(At the apéritif hour, at eleven o'clock, the café experiences a certain liveliness; you can meet artists, writers, newspaper hacks from Montmartre land: Gueldry, painter of the Grenouillière and of boaters; the aquafortist Henri Somm, a delightful conversationalist; Achille Melandri, photographer and novelist; the handsome Michel de l'Hay; the already notorious Mermeix, Henri Pille, the Countess Popo; Hoschédé, who had ruined himself financially, or so everyone amusingly recounts, by having those special trains heated up and readied for his dearly beloved, the painter Gérôme, to ride in; Jean-Louis Forain, whose only thought was to rival Grévin!; the landscape painter, Véron; the painter, Merwarst who was to disappear in the eruption of Mont Pelé; the insufferable Tanzi, the Beziers painter of ponds and pools yelling at every Tom, Dick and Harry in his hoarse voice; the miniaturist, Defeuille; the gay modernist, Goeneutte, the painters Tholer, Faverot; the portrait-painters Paul Quinsac, Antonio de

Anonymous, *Le marché aux modèles*, illustration from a journal. Bibliothèque Nationale, Paris. The market for artists' models, who were mainly Italian, was open on the place Pigalle on Mondays. During the rest of the week, the models could be found in cafés around the place Pigalle.

LA NOUVELLE ATHENES

la Gandara, both former schoolmates of mine; the old painter Bénédict Masson. . . . We must also include Bénassit, the military painter and illustrator, whose words spoken with a comic British accent were bandied about as were those of Forain and Aurélien Scholl. . . .)

It was also at the Nouvelle Athènes, about 1890, that Maurice Ravel met the composer Erik Satie. Ravel was in his early twenties and felt that this meeting strongly influenced him. He considered Satie *"un précurseur maladroit et génial"* (an awkward and inspired precursor) to whom he owed a great deal.[28]

The Nouvelle Athènes was still in existence in 1905 when it was largely frequented by Montmartre inhabitants. Thus, for many years the Nouvelle Athènes was a meeting place for artists, painters and writers ●

LE RAT MORT

The café du Rat Mort, also situated on place Pigalle across from the Nouvelle Athènes, was one of the oldest cafés in the area. Alphonse Daudet boasted that he and the painter Delvau had helped celebrate its opening in 1870 before the days of the Commune.[29] The café was, however, closed during the war and reopened in 1872.

There are several postcards, drawings, paintings and illustrations of the Rat Mort. It was a traditional Second Empire style café with decorative paintings on the walls relating the story of the Rat.

As recounted by many of its habitués, the Rat Mort was more boisterous than the Nouvelle Athènes. In 1872, Verlaine was at the Rat Mort with Rimbaud, and François Porché in *Verlaine tel qu'il fut* relates the following anecdote:

"Un jour au Rat Mort, Rimbaud lui dit: 'Etendez vos mains, je veux vous montrer une expérience.' Aussitôt Rimbaud tirant un couteau de sa poche coupa

— Sans les femmes, qu'est-ce qui nous resterait !...

Dessin de J.-L. Forain.

Left: Jean Louis Forain, *Au Rat, sans les femmes qu'est ce qui nous resterait*, illustration from the *Courrier Français* of December 14, 1890. Musée de Montmartre, Paris. In 1908, the reputation of the Rat Mort had not changed from when it was a meeting place for artists and their models. This illustration translates: "At the Rat, where would we be without women?"

Right: Coll-Toc, *Intérieur du Rat Mort*, illustration from John Grand-Carteret's *Raphael et Gambrinus*, 1886. Musée de Montmartre, Paris. In 1886, the decor of the Rat Mort was still Second Empire: notably, the large mirrors on the walls, the disposition of the tables, and the shape of the light fixtures. This particular atmosphere is captured in certain paintings by Manet and Degas.

LE RAT MORT

Verlaine au poignet. Cros n'eut que le temps de retirer ses mains. Verlaine alors sortit avec son compagnon et sur le trottoir reçut trois autres coups à la cuisse."[30]

(One day at the Rat Mort, Rimbaud told him: "Stretch out your hands. I want to show you an experiment." Rimbaud then took out a knife from his pocket and cut Verlaine on the wrist. Cros had just enough time to pull his own hands away. Verlaine then left with his companion and on the sidewalk was cut three more times on the

thigh.)

In addition, the Rat Mort was the meeting place for artist models when the market for the artist models on the place Pigalle was not open: "*. . . On se montrait le fantôme d'une dame surnommée Fleur de Pipe, qui avait servi de modèle à Balzac et une autre qui se vantait d'avoir couché avec Baudelaire."*[31]

(. . . Someone pointed out the ghost of a woman called Fleur de Pipe who had been used as a model by Balzac and

LE « RAT MORT ». — Dessin de Coll-Toc

Le Vendredi au Rat-Mort. — Raoul Ponchon lisant ses vers.

Heindbrinck, *Le vendredi du Rat Mort avec Raoul Ponchon,* illustration from the *Courrier Français* of March 11, 1888. Musée de Montmartre, Paris. Journalists are gathered around the poet and writer Raoul Ponchon. The Rat Mort did not have its own newspaper as did the Auberge du Clou, the Rochefoucault and the Taverne du Bagne.

LE RAT MORT

another woman who bragged of having slept with Baudelaire.)

Daniel Halévy evokes the atmosphere at the Rat Mort:

"Il me semble que mes parents rapportèrent à table devant moi un de mes impertinents bavardages qui suggéra à Degas cette réponse qui aurait pu être dite au café montmartrois du Rat Mort: 'Il a du vice, il ira loin.'"[32]

(I seem to recall one day at the dinner table my parents repeating an impertinent piece of gossip I had told them. This led Degas to make a remark which could have been overheard at the Rat Mort: "He's a sly dog, he'll go far.")

In the works of Manet and Degas depicting the Rat Mort, women are always featured: *Les deux bockeuses: deux femmes buvant de la bière* (1879, Burrel Collection, Glasgow) or *La Prune* (1878, National Gallery, Washington) or again *Femmes attablées à la terrasse le soir* (1875-1878, Cabinet des Dessins, Musée

801 Montmartre. — La place Pigalle (le Rat mort).

Postcard of the front of the Rat Mort. Musée de Montmartre, Paris. Stained-glass windows embellished the front of the Rat Mort. In the summer, customers sat in front of the café on the sidewalk. The advertising on the store blind announced that the café was open all day and night.

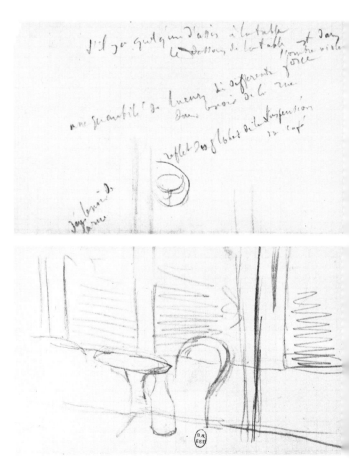

46

du Louvre, Paris). Willette intimates that lesbianism was openly practiced at the Rat Mort.

Manet and his friends frequented at the same time both the Rat Mort and the Nouvelle Athènes. But the more rowdy atmosphere at the Rat Mort bothered them: *"On y crachait dans la bière."*[33] (People even spit in the beer there.) After 1880, they no longer went to the Rat Mort even though Félicien Champsaur claims having seen there at that time: Manet, Degas, Carrier-Belleuse, Cabaner, Tivoli, Goeneutte, Detouche, Paul Alexis, Métra, Vallès, Nadar, Desboutin, and Toupié-Baizié.[34]

After 1880, the regular clientele at the Rat Mort changed as it did at the Nouvelle Athènes. The Rat Mort was now frequented by journalists from the *Courrier Français* and by Montmartre inhabitants. In 1886, an article appeared in the *Courrier Français* in the form of a dialogue between Emile Goudeau and Jules Roques, director of the newspaper. They evoke the names of the habitués at the Rat Mort:

"Willette, Chéret . . . Gambetta aurait déjeuné à la table 6, Courbet au 2, Manet et Desboutin au 8." (Willette, Chéret . . . Gambetta apparently lunched at table number 6, Courbet at number 2, Manet and Desboutin at number 8.)

And they concluded:

" . . . qui fera la synthèse du Rat Mort obtiendrait du même coup l'ensemble de la physionomie de tous les lieux publics de ce pays étrange, extravagant et pourtant lucide qui s'appelle Montmartre."[35]

Au Café du Rat Mort

LE RAT MORT

(. . . Whoever can make a synthesis of the Rat Mort would at the same time have a composite picture of all public places in this strange and extravagant yet lucid land that is called Montmartre.)

Around 1890, the clientele at the Rat Mort evolved again. Besides the journalists from the *Courrier Français*, now writers and painters from the Tambourin, which had closed, could be found there. Thus, a new group gathering around Toulouse-Lautrec was formed with Anquetin, Edouard Dujardin, Conder, and Charles Maurin.

The Rat Mort became an elegant café-restaurant with private rooms that Lautrec depicted in his painting *Le Rat Mort*, Cabinet Particulier, Lucy Jourdain (1899, Courtauld Institute, London).

The Rat Mort was still in existence in 1906 ●

Toulouse-Lautrec, *Le Rat Mort*, oil, 1899. Courtauld Institute Galleries, London. At the Rat Mort, Toulouse-Lautrec met the models and the *"femmes du Rat Mort"* whose company he liked. He also met his friends Conder, Anquetin, Edouard Dujardin, Alfred Stevens, and Charles Maurin there.

LA GRANDE PINTE

Anew type of establishment appeared on the scene when the Grande Pinte opened its doors to the public in 1878. The Grande Pinte's originality was largely due to its decor: *"De grands tables recouvertes de velours d'Utrecht lui donnait un aspect confortable. Les murs de la salle étaient ornés de petits formats. Des vitraux aux fenêtres racontent l'histoire de Panurge.*[36] *Ils sont l'oeuvre d'Henri Pille. . . ."*[37]

(Large tables covered with velvet from Utrecht lent it a cosy appearance. The walls were covered with miniature drawings. The paintings on the windows by Henri Pille, related the story of Panurge.)

The Grande Pinte was situated at 28 avenue Trudaine. It was the first artistic café in Montmartre.

A certain Laplace, proprietor of the Grande Pinte, was both an art dealer and second-hand dealer. He was somewhat eccentric, and on moving into his apartment is believed to have said to his concierge: *"Voici cent sous pour ne jamais me dire bonjour, ni bonsoir."* (Here's a five franc piece for you on the condition that you never wish me good-day or good-night.)

Laplace was fond of art and turned his café into a medieval-style gallery. He had a large art collection and was a familiar face at artists' ateliers.

The Grande Pinte was a favorite meeting place for Manet and his friends in the years 1878 through 1880. There they encountered Montmartre's clamorous youth, who would later frequent the Chat Noir and the Auberge du Clou.

On the walls of his café, Laplace exhibited paintings and drawings; above all,

he was a collector of artists' palettes. A palette painted by Pissarro in 1878 depicts a peasant couple loading a sack of potatoes onto a cart. Overjoyed by the sale of this palette to Laplace, Pissarro was eager to share his good fortune with his friends. He immediately wrote to Monet, explaining how he, too, should go about selling something to Laplace:

"Voyez donc Monsieur Laplace, patron de la grande brasserie place des Martyrs, il vous demandera une palette ornée. J'en ai fait une ainsi que Manet et d'autres. Il m'a payé F. 50 avec difficulté. J'ai tenu bon, je savais qu'il en avait besoin pour sa collection; faites de même et mieux si possible. Si vous voyiez Sisley, faites lui en part et dites lui la situation. Ce serait trop bête de se laisser berner pour si peu."[38]

(Go and see Mr. Laplace, the proprietor of the big brasserie, place des Martyrs; he's sure to ask you for a palette. I've done one and so has Manet and a few others. He paid me fifty francs for it though he was reluctant to part with such a sum. But I held out, I knew he wanted it for his collection. Ask for the same sum or more if possible. If you happen to see Sisley fill him in on the situation. It would be a shame to miss out on such an opportunity.)

Consequently, Manet also painted a palette: *Le Bock sur une palette.*[39] Unfortunately, palettes by other artists remain unknown.

The Grande Pinte was also a meeting place for Montmartre poets and writers. The founder of the Hydropathes,[40] Emile Goudeau, as well as other poets and chansonniers were habitués at the Grande Pinte. It was at this café that Emile

LA GRANDE PINTE

Goudeau and Rodolphe Salis met for the first time.

In the May 14, 1906 issue of *L'Éclair,* Georges Montorgueil recalls this memorable encounter:

"Un soir qu'il montait mélancoliquement la rue des Martyrs, Goudeau s'arrêta à la Grande Pinte (établissement sis avenue Trudaine). Il y était depuis quelques minutes, quand une bande joyeuse fit son entrée: le peintre René Gilbert, le géant Parisel, Forain, Léon Valade. . . . Tout à coup, Gilbert lui désigna un jeune homme robuste, blond fauve qui les accompagnait: 'Tu ne connais pas ce camarade?' 'Non. . . . Vous n'êtes jamais venu aux Hydropathes?' demanda Goudeau au jeune homme.

'Jamais. Je faisais de la peinture à Cernay, loin des rumeurs de la ville. Mais je fonde un cabaret artistique boulevard Rochechouart, 84, voulez-vous assister au dîner d'ouverture?'

'Volontiers.'

Paris 628. **Montmartre. — Cabarets du Clou et de l'Ane-Rouge** (avenue Tru...

Left: Postcard, the front of the Grande Pinte. Musée de Montmartre, Paris. "The Grande Pinte was a place to see many pictures donated by each of the artists and a few of them are of real worth." This annotation is written on a drawing preserved at the Musée Carnavalet.

Right: Coll-Toc, *Intérieur de la Grande Pinte*, Musée de Montmartre, Paris. The Grande Pinte was one of the first cafés to alter its decor. Medieval, rustic or exotic style cafés soon became fashionable, including the Chat Noir, the Auberge du Clou, the Divan Japonais and the Taverne du Bagne.

LA GRANDE PINTE

Le jeune homme fauve, c'était Salis. . . . Le Chat poussant son premier miaulement. Il y en a qui coupent les ponts; Goudeau se bornait à les passer. Désormais, il ferait élection de domicile à Montmartre. Et la gloire de Montmartre lui devait ses plus ardents rayons."

(One evening, walking sadly up rue des Martyrs, Goudeau stopped in at the Grande Pinte. He had only been there for a few moments when a merry crowd came in, the painter René Gilbert, the giant Parisel, Forain, Léon Valade. . . . Suddenly Gilbert pointed out a rugged young man with sandy-colored hair who was with them: 'Do you know our friend over there?'

'No.' Goudeau then turned and asked the young man, 'You've never come to our meetings have you?'

'Never. I used to paint in Cernay, far from the noise of the city. But now I'm going to open up an artistic cabaret on boulevard Rochechouart, number 84; would you like to be present at our

GRANDE PINTE. — Dessin de COLL-TOC.

LA GRANDE PINTE

opening dinner?'

'Yes, with pleasure.'

That lion-haired young man was none other than Salis. The Cat's first meow. There were those who wanted nothing to do with Salis; Goudeau was not one of them. Thereafter, he chose to live in Montmartre. The glory of Montmartre shone even more brightly because of this man Salis.)

The Chat Noir was thus established, and much to the satisfaction of Salis, Goudeau and his friends became regular customers. By 1880 the ambiance in the Grande Pinte radically changed, welcoming those in search of gaiety and fantasy.

Threatened by the popularity of Salis's Chat Noir which opened in 1881, the Grande Pinte was to change yet again. It was rebaptized the Ane Rouge after Laplace sold it to Salis's brother in 1890, and became a refuge for those who were discontented with the celebrated establishment on rue Victor Massé. [41]

A la Grande Pinte, quand le vent
Fait grincer l'enseigne en fer blanc
Alors qu'il gèle
Dans la cuisine on voit briller
Toujours un tronc d'arbre au foyer
Flamme éternelle!

J'attends mes amis . . . au lointain.
Tout est gelé sur les chemins
La plaine est grise.
Pour mieux voir, j'ouvre les rideaux
Le givre étend sur les carreaux
Un train de glace;
Il trace des monts, des forêts,
Des lacs, des fleurs et des cyprès:
Je les efface!

Nous sommes quatre compagnons
Qui buvons bien, mais sommes bons,
Dieu nous pardonne!
L'un mort, il en restera trois,
Puis deux, puis un, et puis je crois
Après . . . Personne!

Rodolphe Darzens
Nuits à Paris

(When the wind rattles the white iron signboard
When it is bitter cold outside
There is always
A blazing fire in the kitchen at the Grande Pinte
Eternal flame!

I await my friends . . . in the distance
The paths are frozen over
The plane is a dismal gray
I open the curtains to see more clearly
The window panes are covered with frost
A trail of ice outlining mountains,
Forests, lakes, flowers and cypress trees
I erase them!

Four friends are we
Hearty drinkers but good men
God forgive us
One of us dead, three left, then another
And yet another and then . . . No one!) ●

LA ROCHEFOUCAULT

Along with the Rat Mort, the café La Rochefoucault was one of the oldest cafés in Montmartre. It existed long before the Commune, and the Goncourts recall having been dragged there by Aurélien Scoll in 1861:

"Un vilain salon de café où les gens contre les murs jouent à la bouillotte." [42] (A shabby café where people sit against the walls playing cards.)

It was here at the café La Rochefoucault that the Goncourts met *"cette basse bohème"* they so despised, those literary and artistic youths claiming adherence to the naturalistic school of Champfleury and Murger.

No paintings, sketches or illustrations of this café exist today. Only Gabriel Astruc's descriptions in *Pavillon des fantômes* [43] and Henri Gervex's *Souvenirs* [44] enable us to imagine what the decor was like:

"Une salle carrée garnie de banquettes de moleskine verte et d'une

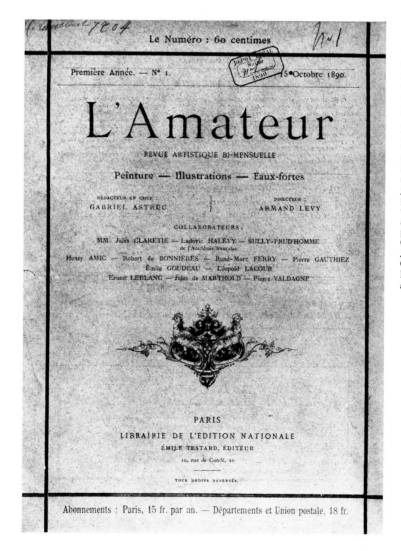

Le Numéro : 60 centimes

Première Année. — N° 1. 15 Octobre 1890.

L'Amateur

REVUE ARTISTIQUE BI-MENSUELLE

Peinture — Illustrations — Eaux-fortes

RÉDACTEUR EN CHEF :
GABRIEL ASTRUC

DIRECTEUR :
ARMAND LEVY

COLLABORATEURS :

MM. Jules CLARETIE — Ludovic HALÉVY — SULLY-PRUD'HOMME
de l'Académie française

Henry AMIC — Robert de BONNIÈRES — René-Marc FERRY — Pierre GAUTHIEZ
Émile GOUDEAU — Léopold LACOUR
Ernest LEBLANC — Jules de MARTHOLD — Pierre VALDAGNE

PARIS
LIBRAIRIE DE L'ÉDITION NATIONALE
ÉMILE TESTARD, ÉDITEUR
10, rue de Condé, 10

TOUS DROITS RÉSERVÉS.

Abonnements : Paris, 15 fr. par an. — Départements et Union postale, 18 fr.

L'Amateur, a bi-monthly newspaper published from October 15, 1890 to January 15, 1891. Département des Imprimés, Bibliothèque Nationale, Paris. This art journal was not a humorous or satirical publication but rather a periodical vulgarizing works of art. There were seven issues of which only six are known. The journal was to be printed every two weeks. Each issue was a monograph on one painter: Raphael Collin, Charles Jacques, Henri Gervex, Gérome, Norbert Goeneutte, and Cormon.

LA ROCHEFOUCAULT

quinzaine de tables de marbre permettant de traiter soixante personnes environ. Un escalier en colimaçon conduisant au billard, peu fréquenté d'ailleurs car le café 'La Roche' était avant tout une académie de dominos. Les joueurs ne plaisantaient pas."

(A square room furnished with green moleskin wall-sofas and about fifteen marble tables with seating for approximately sixty people. A spiral staircase leading to the billiard room, rarely used because the café "La Roche" was first and foremost a school of dominos. The players did not joke around.)

Gabriel Astruc relates that two teams sat down at a table to one side of the café: *"Le père Léonard, grand violoniste virtuose des concerts classiques, Henry Dupray, peintre militaire de la lignée des Meissonnier, le Commandant d'Arfeuille et comme quatrième Henri Gervex, Pierre Carrier-Balleuse ou l'éditeur Lemoine et à une autre table Fernand Cormon, Charles Jacque, le graveur Lionel Lecoulteux et le docteur Demay."*

(Old Léonard, the great classical violin virtuoso, Henry Dupray, military painter after the style of Meissonier, the commandant of Arfeuille and the fourth player, Henri Gervex, Pierre Carrier-Belleuse or the editor Lemoine. At another table Fernand Cormon, Charles Jacque, the engraver Lionel Lecoulteux and the doctor Demay.)

The Rochefoucault was also a café where painters would get together for discussions. To one side of these domino players sat Degas, conversing with Forain and Lautrec; they also listened while Guy de Maupassant explained his conception of literature and spoke to them of Flaubert.

"La Roche" was more Degas's territory, although Manet began to go there towards 1873. It was there that Manet probably met Alfred Stevens, who had this to say of Manet's painting, *Le Bon Bock:* "My dear Manet, you have a fine piece of work there, but allow me to make only one comment. Your Bon Bock isn't drinking beer from Strasbourg but beer from Haarlem." [45]

In 1890 the habitués of "La Roche" decided to publish a magazine, *L'Amateur.* [46] Charles Jacque hoped that by printing facsimiles of his etchings in this magazine he would create interest among subscribers in his original engravings.

One year later, in 1891, a shadow theatre was set up in the cellar at "La Roche." Unfortunely it was short lived and its repertory remains unknown.

It is difficult indeed to say much more about the ambiance at La Rochefoucault. Historians know very little about this café despite its own illustrated magazine and a few shadow theatre performances. Above all, the Rochefoucault was a café frequented by artists and critics seeking a little amusement and perhaps a game of billiards or dominos.

Although the atmosphere at the Rochefoucault had never been recreated in any paintings or sketches, Léon Gandillot chose this café as a setting for his play *Vers l'Amour.* [47]

The café Rochefoucault, however, was not as famous as it should have been. It deserves to be ranked among the celebrated cafés in the place Pigalle ●

LE TAMBOURIN

The Tambourin on 62 boulevard Clichy was a café frequented, for the most part, by painters. Its existence was brief–from 1885 to 1887.

The Tambourin was run by an Italian, "La Segatori." Gauguin informs us that she was *"très belle malgré son âge"* (very beautiful despite her age) and with whom Van Gogh *"était très amoureux"* (was very much in love).[48]

According to John Grand-Carteret, the Tambourin opened on April 10, 1885 with an exhibition of paintings and tambourins which, a month later, were put up for public sale. "Paintings and tambourins by Gérôme, François Clairin, Dantan, Hagborg, Février, Dupray, Pille, Benjamin Constant, Besnard, Barrias, Mazerolle, Bogolouboff. . . . "[49]

When Van Gogh was in Paris in 1887, all his paintings had apparently been sold and for this reason he accepted to decorate the café "gratis." We have no knowledge as to what these paintings

Toulouse-Lautrec, *La gueule de bois*, oil, 1889. Fogg Art Museum, Boston. This painting is of Suzanne Valadon who Lautrec had known for several years. The setting could be at the Tambourin or, as the Tambourin closed in 1889, at the Rat Mort where Valadon first met Renoir, Puvis de Chavannes, and Lautrec.

LE TAMBOURIN

represented nor do we know exactly where they were hung in the Tambourin, on the ground floor or upstairs.

Van Gogh kept himself very busy at the Tambourin. In 1886-1887, together with Lautrec, Anquetin and Besnard, he organized a second exhibition there. In a letter to his brother Théo he wrote how happy he was to have organized this event: *"Besnard y a vendu son premier tableau, Anquetin y a vendu une étude, moi ayant fait l'échange avec Gauguin, tous, nous avons eu quelque chose."*[50] (Besnard sold his first painting, Anquetin a study, and myself, I made an exchange with Gauguin. We all got something.)

Nevertheless, his efforts to sell these paintings were, on the whole, unsuccessful, and all the works were put up for public sale at the Hôtel Drouot.

During this period (1886), Gauguin painted two tambourins: *Fleurs et feuillages* and *Fruits.* These were more than likely a part of Van Gogh's exhibition. Despite the

Coll-Toc, *Intérieur du Tambourin,* illustration from *Raphael et Gambrinus,* 1886. Musée de Montmartre, Paris. The decor had an Italian theme. The serving girls and Agostina Segatori wore Italian costumes. The tables were tambourins, the plates were porcelain tambourins, the lantern was a glass tambourin—there were tambourins everywhere.

LE TAMBOURIN. — Dessin de COLL-TOC.

exhibition's misfortune, Van Gogh carried on with his work out of love for the "beautiful Segatori." [51] He then organized an exhibition of *"crépons qui a influencé Anquetin et Besnard"* (an exhibition of crepons that influenced Anquetin and Besnard). This exhibition, too, ended in failure.

The Tambourin counted Lautrec among its faithful habitués. There, he painted a portrait of Van Gogh sitting at a table, buried in thought, with a glass in front of him. [52] It is probable that Lautrec also did a portrait of Suzanne Valadon there whom he had met in 1885: *La gueule de bois.*

The Tambourin's bad reputation led to its ruin. Gauguin relates that: *"La police à plusieurs reprises a dû intervenir pour des affaires: Pausini et Prado."* (The police had to intervene many times because of the Pausini and Prado trouble.) We have no way of knowing whether these disturbances were caused by criminal acts or simply by brawls. Van Gogh intimates that Segatori was not free to do as she pleased and that she was apparently influenced and controlled by an unknown man. [53]

Advertisements in *La Gazette du Bagne*, such as the one below in 1885, led one to believe the Tambourin would have a brilliant career. However, this was not to be.

Au Tambourin
-Rien des auberges dont la nudité et le délabrement des murs fait la pauvre originalité.
-Rien des cafés prétentieux, dont les plafonds vous assomment et dont les ors vous aveuglent.
Au Tambourin
-C'est un bien retiro chaud, plutôt musée que café, musée qui trahit, dans son agencement l'intervention et la direction d'une femme de goût.
-C'est en effet Madame Agostina Segatori, propriétaire du Tambourin qui a réuni, classé, placé avec un sentiment artistique, les oeuvres de maître qui ont transformé son établissement en une des plus intéressantes galeries de tableaux qui se puisse.
-Pour ajouter encore à l'attrait de son établissement, la directrice s'est adjointe les plus charmantes collaboratrices qui se puissent voir, fraîches fleurs écloses au soleil d'Italie et épanouies dans le rayonnement chaud de notre capitale.

(At the Tambourin you'll find none of those bare and delapidated walls that account for the poor originality in most inns. You'll find nothing in common with those pretentious cafés whose gilded ceilings leave you blinded and senseless. It is a cosy little corner, more museum than café, revealing in its decor the touch of a woman of taste. It is indeed Madame Agostina Segatori, proprietress of the Tambourin, who has brought together, sorted and hung with artistic feeling the works of masters, transforming her establishment into one of the most interesting art galleries in existence. To enhance her café even more, Madame Segatori has engaged the most charming young ladies you'd ever hope to see, fresh-blown flowers budding in the Italian sun and blossoming in the warm radiance of our capital.) ●

LE CHAT NOIR

In 1881 the Chat Noir opened at 84 boulevard Rochechouart near the Elysée-Montmartre. It then moved to 12 rue de Laval in 1885 (today rue Victor Massé).[54]

Rodolphe Salis, the celebrated founder of the Chat Noir, attracted a large following. At first the poets and chansonniers, who were formerly members of the Hydropathes: Emile Goudeau, their front-rank man, Mac Nab, Rollinat, Harancourt, Georges Lorin, Camille de Sainte Croix, Marcel Legay, Sapeck, Raoul Ponchon, Jules Jouy. In no time they were joined by other poets, painters and musicians from Montmartre: Willette, Steinlen, Uzès, Fau. . . .

The atmosphere at the cabaret was very lighthearted. Poets recited their poems and chansonniers sang their verses, with occasional accompaniment on the piano.

Jules Jouy sang *Les Grevy, Le Bouton de Culotte* or *l'Exécution,* Victor Meusy

Right: Anonymous, *Intérieur du deuxième Chat Noir,* illustration. Musée de Montmartre, Paris. The customers could choose to sit at tables in different rooms, each pompously named. Beer was served and, at dinner time, French fries, which everyone ate with their fingers. The decor was the same as that at the first Chat Noir with paintings on the walls by the habitués.

Far right: Henri Pille, *L'Ancien Chat Noir,* illustration from the *Almanach du Figaro,* 1884. Musée de Montmartre, Paris. Seated at the table in front, Henri Rivière is easily recognizable; behind him, Willette is reading his newspaper. On the mantlepiece are all the unusual objects that Salis fancied.

Théophile Steinlen, *Henri Rivière,* pencil drawing. Cabinet des Dessins, Musée du Louvre, Paris. Salis handed over the production of the shadow theatre to Henri Rivière who, in turn, became its art director. He was responsible for most of the sets created at the Chat Noir.

Right: Paul Merwarst, *La façade du deuxième Chat Noir,* drawing. Musée Carnavalet, Paris. On the front of this former private residence, already decorated by Henri Pille, Salis added two lanterns by Grasset and above the door a sign by Willette. He also affixed a huge terracotta cat standing in front of a radiant sun to hide the middle window on the first floor.

LE CHAT NOIR

sang *Les Halles, Les Choux.*

Alphonse Allais and Léon Bloy also frequented the Chat Noir, as did Marie Krysinska who created new musical rhythms to accompany poems by Verlaine and Charles Cros. Albert Tinchant, Charles de Sivry and Georges Fragerolles are some of the pianists who played there every evening.

In 1884 Charles Cros became a regular customer at the cabaret, bringing along with him Verlaine and Mallarmé.

Aristide Bruant also became a frequent patron of the Chat Noir in 1884, however his aggressive and vulgar manner shocked the other habitués. Nevertheless Bruant's composition, *Le Chat Noir,* became the cabaret's theme song:

Je cherche fortune
Autour du Chat Noir
Au clair de la lune
A Montmartre,

Je cherche fortune

INTÉRIEUR DU CHAT NOIR. — Dessin de Fernand Fau.

L'ANCIEN CHAT NOIR, BOULEVARD ROCHECHOUART.

Left: Poster announcing the shadow theatre program. Musée de Montmartre, Paris. The frame depicting the cat holding his tail was done by Henri Rivière. For each new show, the text inside would be changed.

Right: Théophile Steinlen, *Le Chat Noir en tournée*, poster, 1896. Musée de Montmartre, Paris. Steinlen drew this famous cat when the shadow theatre company went on tour throughout France and abroad.

Far right: Henri Pille, *En tête du journal du Chat Noir*, Musée de Montmartre, Paris. The newspaper appeared every Saturday from January 14, 1882 until May 30, 1895. Henri Pille designed the logo which remained the same throughout the journal's entire existence, with only two or three exceptions.

THÉÂTRE DU Chat Noir

Rideau à 9 h. 1/4 — 12, Rue Victor-Massé

EXCEPTIONNELLEMENT
CE SOIR VENDREDI SAINT
LA
MARCHE A L'ÉTOILE

Mystère en 10 tableaux, poème et Musique
De GEORGES FRAGEROLLE
Dessins de Henri RIVIÈRE

LE SPHINX

Épopée Légendaire en SEIZE Tableaux
Poème et Musique de *GEORGES FRAGEROLLE* — Dessins de *A. VIGNOLA*
Le Récitant, M. G. FRAGEROLLE — *Piano*, M. COLOMB

INTERMÈDES, CHANSONS et VERS HUMORISTIQUES
INTERPRÉTÉS PAR LES AUTEURS
Jean GOUDEZKI, Gabriel MONTOYA, CHARTON
Jehan RICTUS, JOYEUX, etc.
Présentés par R. SALIS

Le Bureau de Location est ouvert de 11 h. à 8 h., 12, rue Victor-Massé.

LE CHAT NOIR

Autour du Chat Noir
Au clair de la lune
A Montmartre, le soir.

(I seek my fortune
At the Black Cat
In the moonlight
Of Montmartre,

I seek my fortune
At the Black Cat
In the moonlight
Of Montmartre, in the evening.)

From the moment the cabaret opened in January 1881 until March 1895, Salis published a weekly newspaper, *Le Chat Noir*. The four pages *in folio* contained poems, stories, tales about café life, write-ups on contemporary artists, reviews of exhibitions and some advertising on the back page. This paper became a uniting factor for all the habitués at the Chat Noir.

Every week the paper's front page would carry humorous drawings and

LE CHAT NOIR

caricatures, usually drawn by Caran d'Ache, Steinlen, Uzès, Rivière, Fau, Does, Ferdinandus and Willette.

In June 1885 Salis decided to move; the cabaret had become too small and was too near the popular balls held at the Elysée-Montmartre. He moved into a private residence on rue Laval and there set up a new cabaret. The move was not without its mishaps and adventures.

With three floors at his disposal Salis gradually fixed up a number of rooms. To each room he assigned a pompous name: Salle des Seigneurs, Salle du Conseil, Salle des Etats, Oratoire, and the Salle de Fêtes. Salis decorated the walls with paintings and sketches by the cabaret's habitués, thus acquiring a splendid collection that he catalogued in *Le Chat Noir Guide*. He commissioned Willette to do a stained-glass design for the bay window on the ground floor and named it *Le Veau d'Or*. [55]

The Chat Noir became a cabaret where Parisian high society was seen and a

LE CHAT NOIR

Henri Rivière, *84 boulevard Rochechouart,* illustration from the *Chat Noir,* June 13, 1885. Musée de Montmartre, Paris. The cabaret was located in an old post office; there were two large rooms, separated by a curtain. The first room was reserved for clients, while the second was a rendezvous point for all the habitués. This room was called the "Institute." Drawings by Henri Pille, Gandara, Henri Rivière, Puvis de Chavannes and Carolus Duran were hung on the walls. In this drawing, the atmosphere at the first Chat Noir is recreated: the crowd on the sidewalk, the signboard designed by Willette, and the fireplace with all its bric-a-brac.

Far left: Anonymous, *Salis bonimentant,* ca. 1885. Musée de Montmartre, Paris. Every evening Salis presided over the gatherings at the Chat Noir, and would always introduce his poets with great ado: "Silence, listen to him, a genius is in your midst."

Left: Anonymous, *Steinlen,* from *Hommes d'aujourd'hui,* Musée de Montmartre, Paris. Steinlen was the greatest contributor to the *Chat Noir Journal.*

DESSIN DE HENRI RIVIÈRE

new generation of poets and chansonniers was heard, such as Xavier Privas, Gabriel Montoya, Pierre Trimouillat, Jehan Rictus, Vincent Hyspa, Maurice Donnay, the singers Yvette Guilbert, and Thereza.[56]

Salis also proposed a new attraction: the shadow theatre. Salis let Henri Rivière run the theatre. The performances were held in the Salle des Fêtes on the second floor. Forty-three plays in all, written by nineteen artists were performed from 1887 to 1896 at the Chat Noir. Some were

historical plays such as *1808* and *L'Epopée* by Caran d'Ache; others were mystical and religious, *La Marche à l'Etoile* by Henri Rivière; and still others were comedies of manners such as *Pauvre Pierrot, Carnaval de Venise, Flagrant Délit*.

With repeated performances, techniques were gradually improved upon and became more intricate. In the wings, wind and rain effects were produced. At first, background music was solely provided by a pianist. In later performances, the

Above: Paul Merwarst, *La salle des fêtes pendant la représentation de l'Epopée*, drawing, 1886. Musée Carnavalet, Paris. This room was packed every evening at the Chat Noir. In the picture, Merwarst painted Francisque Sarcey, Alphonse Daudet, Emile Zola, Mac Nab, Rodolphe Salis, General Boulanger, and himself, among the members of the audience.

Right: Georges Redon, *Les coulisses du Théâtre d'Ombres*, 1890. Musée de Montmartre, Paris. The stage hands at these performances were habitués, poets, and chansonniers from the Chat Noir. As time went on and the techniques became more complicated, additional helpers were needed to manipulate the sets.

pianist was joined by a singer or even a chorus. [57]

By 1892 Salis had grown weary. He bought Naintré Château near Châtellerault, his home town, and decided to retire there. He wanted to sell the paper *Le Chat Noir* and at the same time to sell his lease. His only desire was to keep the shadow theatre going and stage productions in France and abroad.

During a performance in Châteaudun in 1897 Salis fell seriously ill. Salis had just enough time to return home to Naintré where he died a few days later.

His art collection was auctioned off between 1897 and 1904. With the death of Salis, the Chat Noir closed its doors ●

Left, above: Adolphe Willette, *Pierrot amoureux*, illustration from the *Chat Noir Journal*, April 8, 1822. Musée de Montmartre, Paris. A few of Willette's drawings were published by Léon Vannier in 1884 in a collection entitled *Pauvre Pierrot*.

Left, below: Théophile Steinlen, *Les chats*, illustration from the *Chat Noir Journal*, May 4, 1884. Musée de Montmartre, Paris. One of Steinlen's 83 illustrations which appeared in the *Chat Noir Journal*. After the Chat Noir cabaret closed, some of these drawings were regrouped and published by Flammarion in 1903.

Left: Uzès, *L'Entrée de Salis dans la bonne rue de Laval*, drawing, 1885. Musée de Chatellerault, Paris. Salis moved out of his cabaret during the night of June 10, 1885 between eleven o'clock and midnight. The event was quite a masquerade: "My two grooms in short pants led the parade, followed by our golden banner with its sable coat. . . . Then my majordomo dressed as a sub-prefect who, in a very dignified manner, controlled the curious spectators, ordering the amazed passers-by: 'Keep out of the way . . .'" Salis wore a prefect's costume, a sword at his side.

Horrible fin d'un Poisson rouge, par Steinlen.

L'AUBERGE DU CLOU

The Auberge du Clou opened in December 1883, at 30 avenue Trudaine, next door to the Grande Pinte.

The originality of the Auberge du Clou was due to its decor more than anything else. The proprietor, Paul Thomaschet,[58] from the canton of Grisons in Switzerland, wanted to imbue the café with a country-like atmosphere, thus setting it apart from the other cafés and cabarets in Montmartre at that time. The waiters were attired as countryfolk, the walls covered with naif art and paintings depicting traditional scenes, such as *Le Juif Errant* and *Mort à crédit*, and an assortment of bric-a-brac filled the place. The coat pegs in the hall were shaped like nails.

Thomaschet opened up a large room on the first floor where lunches and dinners were served. He asked Willette to do a series of nine paintings for this room, *Le bon aubergiste, La mariée, Le souper, Les*

cerises, *La veuve de Pierrot*, *L'Eau*, *Le vin*, *Le punch* and *La bière*. Willette chose Pierrot and drink as themes for these paintings.

In his memoirs, *Feu Pierrot*, Willette writes that he received 3000 francs for his labor. He worked at the Auberge in the mornings before lunching with his friends. His companion, Christine, took it upon herself to help out by twisting Japanese crepons around the gilded chandeliers.

"C'est dommage car les crépons représentaient de belles compositions et me revenaient fort chers; et c'est également fâcheux parce que le crépitement de couleurs vives faisait tort aux peintures de tons gris." 59

(What a pity, because those crepons were beautiful compositions and cost me quite a lot of money. It is also regrettable because their crackling bright colors do an injustice to the grey tones in my paintings.)

Japanese crepons were very fashionable in Paris in 1887 and 1888. If

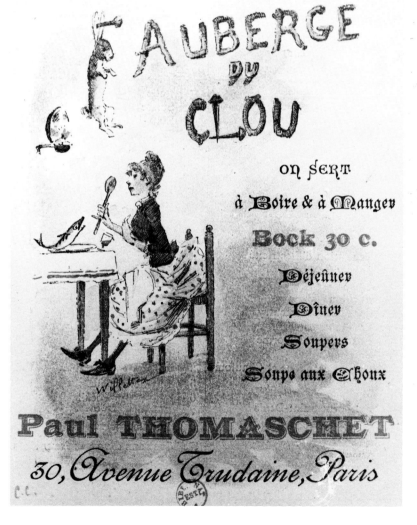

Adolphe Willette, *Menu de l'Auberge du Clou*, Musée de Montmartre, Paris.

Left: Paul Merwarst, *Façade de la Grande Pinte et de l'Auberge du Clou*, drawing, 1886. Musée Carnavalet, Paris.

L'AUBERGE DU CLOU

Willette found them costly, Van Gogh on the contrary, found them very reasonable. [60]

In 1892 Thomaschet renovated the cellar where he set up a shadow theatre. On opening night two plays were performed, *La Styliste* by Henri de Weindel with scenery by Miguel Utrillo (believed to be Maurice Utrillo's father) and *Un Noël*, scenery by Utrillo and music by Satie. [61] The decor in the cellar thus changed and apparently several paintings or frescoes appeared on the walls. In *Nuits à Paris*, Rodolphe Darzens described these paintings:

> *"Les plus abracadabrantes folies dûes à l'imagination en délire de trois peintres de talent: Henri Rivière, Henri Somm, Adolphe Willette."* [62]

(Three very talented painters, Henri Rivière, Henri Somm, and Adolphe Willette, have created through the delirious wanderings of their imagination the finest abracadraba madness.)

Adolphe Willette, four oil paintings, ca. 1885. Private Collection. Women and drink—themes dear to Willette—are the subjects of these paintings done in grey tonalities. Clockwise from upper left: *Le bon aubergiste. La mariée. Le souper, Les cerises.*

Right: Anonymous, *Intérieur de l'Auberge du Clou*, illustration. Musée de Montmartre, Paris. Portrayed here is the famous wooden staircase leading to the upper floor where Willette's paintings could be seen.

L'AUBERGE DU CLOU

John Grand-Carteret identified the paintings: *La nativité de Victor Hugo, Une femme au cochon* by Henri Somm, *Guillotine et champs de bataille, Croque-mort, Convoi funèbre, Drame au fond de la mer, Attaque nocturne,* and the last painting, *Une femme qui cloue son coeur au clou et qui s'en va cette héroïque action accomplie* (A woman who nails her heart on a nail and departs after carrying out this heroic act).[63] In French, there is a double meaning for *au clou,* in which case the translation would read: A woman who sells her heart at a pawn shop and departs after carrying out this heroic act.

These paintings were probably completed between 1883 and 1885. They were replaced ten years later by paintings of a very different style, *Une femme au parapluie, Un bruant* and *Un tête d'homme.*[64]

The atmosphere at the Clou was very different from that at the Chat Noir. Thomaschet was not the literary and

69

L'AUBERGE DU CLOU

artistic man Salis was. Who in fact frequented the Clou? Certainly all those who were unhappy with Salis's new Chat Noir on rue Victor Massé, especially since that cabaret now attracted Parisian high society. However, a number of poets, artists and painters remained faithful to the Chat Noir, although they also went to the Auberge du Clou. Willette, who was one of them, happened to be sitting in front of the Clou when Salis moved out of the Chat Noir. Nevertheless, the Clou was favored above all by some, such as Courteline, Alphonse Allais and the painter Bottini.

The Clou was the scene of Debussy's first encounter with Erik Satie: "I (Erik) was drawn towards him (Debussy) and yearned to be at his side constantly." [65] Former bandmaster at the Chat Noir, Satie was engaged as pianist at the Clou. However it would be more accurate to say that Satie influenced Debussy. Cocteau also describes a first encounter between the two musicians:

Augustin Grass-Mick, *Erik Satie à la terrasse de l'Auberge du Clou,* drawing, 1892. Private Collection. Bandmaster at the Chat Noir, Erik Satie was afterwards engaged as pianist at the Clou. There he met Courteline.

Right: Miguel Utrillo, *Le Théâtre d'Ombres,* poster. Musée National d'Art Moderne Paris. Like the Chat Noir, the Clou had its own shadow theatre. Satie and Utrillo created a play there. Satie composed the music while Utrillo provided the scenery. Unfortunately, this play has been lost.

Far right: Anonymous, *Femme au parapluie,* oil. Private Collection. Paris. This painting, along with the other three at present in the cellar at the Auberge du Clou, has never been reproduced. Unfortunately, we do not know who the artist was.

L'AUBERGE DU CLOU

"Un soir, Erik Satie et Claude Debussy sont à la même table. Ils se plaisent. Satie demande à Debussy ce qu'il prépare. Debussy composait comme tout le monde une Wagnerie avec Catulle Mendès; Satie fait la grimace. Croyez-moi, murmura-t-il, assez de Wagner! C'est beau mais pas de nous . . . "

Then speaking of Pelléas's aesthetic:

"Il faudrait que l'orchestre ne grimace pas quand un personnage entre en scène. Est-ce que les arbres du décor grimacent? Il faudrait faire un décor musical, créer un climat musical où les personnages bougent et causent, pas de couplets, pas de leitmotiv, se servir d'une certaine atmosphère Puvis de Chavannes."

(One evening Erik Satie and Claude Debussy were sitting at the same table. They liked each other's company. Satie asked Debussy what he was composing at the time. Like everyone else, Debussy, with Catulle Mendès, was composing something Wagnerian. Satie made a face. Believe you

L'AUBERGE DU CLOU

me, he muttered, enough of Wagner! It's beautiful but not *our* Wagnerian compositions. . . . Do the trees on the stage make faces? You have to create a musical setting, a musical atmosphere in which the characters move and talk, no verses, no leitmotiv, you must use a certain Puvis de Chavannes type atmosphere.)

When Thomaschet retired to his native Grisons in 1897, the Auberge du Clou was sold. The cabaret became a haunt for journalists from the *Vache Enragée*, a Montmartre newspaper ●

AUBERGE «DU CLOU». — Dessin de COLL-TOC.

LA TAVERNE DU BAGNE

The Taverne du Bagne on 2 boulevard de Clichy and opposite the Cirque Fernando, was one of the most original cafés in Paris.

Since it resembled no other café, the Taverne du Bagne is difficult to classify either as an artistic and literary café or as an establishment where one would go simply to have a good time, as was the case at the Ciel, the Néant or the Enfer.

The Taverne du Bagne opened and was managed by Maxime Lisbonne, a former convict and Communard who had a gift for infusing each of his cafés with a very particular ambiance. [66] The Bagne only lasted six months. It opened on October 6, 1885, and the invitations to the opening were singular: *"A minuit et demi, citoyen, tu es invité à venir à la Taverne du Bagne, 2 boulevard de Clichy, manger la soupe canaque et les gourganes de Toulon.* [67] *Salut et Fraternité. Signé: Lisbonne.* (At half past midnight, citizen,

Right: Anonymous, *Portrait de Maxime Lisbonne.* Musée de Montmartre, Paris. "Lisbonne, ex-Communard Is truly a lucky devil I am, to please the public. That's his business!"

Far right: Coll-Toc, *Intérieur de la Taverne de Bagne,* illustration. Musée de Montmartre, Paris. "A sort of prison refectory, lit by oil lamps, such as can be seen in small far-away train stations, and on the walls, paintings of the Commune, men and things, all of it smeared across meters . . ." —From *Raphael et Gambrinus.*

Left: Coll-Toc, *Intérieur de l'Auberge du Clou,* illustration from *Raphael et Gambrinus.* Musée de Montmartre, Paris. The interior of the Auberge du Clou was thus described: "Small window panes draped with red curtains made from cotton, rustic fireplaces and staircases, furniture in the same style, half-timbered ceilings, stoneware plates and pictures in wooden frames.

LA TAVERNE DU BAGNE

Dimanche 8 Novembre 1885   N° 2. — 10 Centimes.

GAZETTE DU BAGNE

RÉDACTION	RÉDACTEUR EN CHEF	ADMINISTRATION
2, Boulevard de Clichy, 2	Maxime LISBONNE	2, Boulevard de Clichy, 2
Cellule R		Cellule A

LOUISE MICHEL

Il semble qu'il n'y ait qu'à laisser courir la plume pour raconter la vie de cette femme, grande, entre toutes, par l'esprit, par le savoir, par l'énergie et par le dévouement.

Nous aurions voulu raconter Louise Michel dans l'entraînement chaud de nos souvenirs.

Mais nous nous sommes trouvé arrêtés par un scrupule :

Non-seulement Louise Michel, cette héroïne, a vécu nos luttes et nos souffrances; non-seulement elle a été la plus énergique dans le combat et la plus fière, comme la plus patiente dans l'épreuve : mais elle s'est élevée, personnification rayonnante de la Révolution, par tant d'actes d'un dévouement sublime, que, pour ménager sa modestie, et, d'autre part, pour ne pas être taxés d'exagération dans notre éloge, en nous laissant aller à notre admiration, nous avons voulu céder, pour un jour, la parole au froid écrivain biographe de la grande citoyenne dans le dictionnaire de Larousse. Voici :

« Louise Michel, institutrice française, née en 1835. Elle était institutrice aux Batignolles lorsque, à la fin de l'Empire, elle s'occupa de politique et des questions sociales mises à l'ordre du jour par l'Internationale.

» Douée d'une imagination vive, Louise Michel fut vivement affectée par les évènements du siège de Paris et commença alors à montrer une grande exaltation.

» Lors du mouvement du 18 mars, elle prit un costume de garde-national et, armée d'une carabine, elle se dirigea vers le lieu où la lutte venait de s'engager.

» Après la rupture entre la Commune de Paris et l'Assemblée de Versailles, Louise Michel organisa le Comité central de l'Union des femmes, présida le club de la Révolution tenu à l'église Saint-Bernard, et prononça des discours ardents dans divers autres clubs. En même temps, elle envoyait des articles au Cri du Peuple, se rendait au fort d'Issy et était blessée en prenant part à la défense.

» Rentrée à Paris, elle déploya jusqu'à la fin de la lutte, la plus grande énergie et fut arrêtée quelque temps après l'entrée des troupes de Versailles à Paris.

» Traduite le 16 décembre 1871 devant le 6e conseil de guerre, Louise Michel déclara qu'elle ne voulait pas se défendre, qu'elle appartenait tout entière à la Révolution sociale et qu'elle avait participé à l'incendie de Paris. — « Je voulais, dit-elle, opposer une barrière de flammes aux envahisseurs de Versailles », et elle ajouta : « Un jour j'ai proposé à Ferré d'envahir l'Assemblée. Je voulais deux victimes : M. Thiers et moi, car j'avais fait le sacrifice de ma vie ; j'étais décidée à frapper. »

» En terminant, elle demanda la mort ; et s'adressant au Conseil :

» — Si vous n'êtes pas des lâches, s'écria-t-elle, tuez-moi. »

» Condamnée à la déportation dans une enceinte fortifiée, Louise Michel fut dirigée sur la Nouvelle-Calédonie.

« On a d'elle un recueil de contes, légendes et historiettes à l'usage des enfants, le Livre du jour de l'an (1872), publié au profit de sa mère et qui, dans son genre, n'est pas sans mérite.

you are invited to the Taverne du Bagne, 2 boulevard de Clichy, for *canaque* soup and *gourganes* from Toulon. Greetings and Fraternity. Signed: Lisbonne.)

The interior of the Bagne was decorated with paintings alluding to the lives of convicts and soldiers: the aborted escape of Jeanne and Magnier; Lisbonne bidding his country farewell; Rochefort—in black dress—a modern day Moses saved from the floods; *Ferrement de Maroteau;* Olivier Pain before his execution by an English firing squad; and portraits of Fortin, Alphonse Humbert, Pierre Broussat, and Rocques de Filhol as convicts. Illustrations published in the tavern's newspaper, the *Gazette du Bagne,* are all that remain of these paintings.

The café was immediately successful. People lined up to get into the café. From inside, Maxime Lisbonne would shout: *"Faites entrer une nouvelle fournée de condamnés!"* (Let another bunch of convicts in!) Inside the café, a release pass was issued to each person for his good conduct and his hearty drinking. Lisbonne would let them leave and then shout: *"Les libérés peuvent passer au Greffe et s'en aller."* (The newly freed prisoners can go to the office of the clerk of the Court and depart.)[68]

The waiters were dressed as convicts

LA TAVERNE DU BAGNE

in green stocking caps and red jackets and pants with ball and chain attached to their feet. They would offer the *forcénés* (the frenzied crowd) a *Nouméa* which was absinthe, or a *boulet* (canon ball) which was a tankard of beer.

"*Citoyens entre Paris et Montmartre, à mi-montée des Martyrs, l'ex-forçat Maxime Lisbonne vient de ressusciter et de résumer le Bagne. C'est une hardiesse et une curiosité uniques dans l'histoire des fantaisies qui ont rendu fameuse la butte chère aux parisiens. C'est la Taverne du Bagne.*" (From *La Gazette du Bagne*)

(Citizens from Paris to Montmartre, half way up rue des Martyrs, the ex-convict Maxime Lisbonne has just been brought back to life and started up again the Bagne. An audacious and curious place, unique in the annals of fantasy, that has already made famous the butte cherished by Parisians. It is the Taverne du Bagne.) ●

L'ABBAYE DE THELEME

Situated on place Pigalle next to the Rat Mort and the Nouvelle Athènes, the Abbaye de Thélème, created as a Rabelaisian cenacle, was a literary rather than an artistic café. *"Les thélémistes ont l'honneur de vous inviter à fêter François Rabelais en inaugurant son Abbaye de Thélème, 1 place Pigalle, sous la présidence de leur vénérable Prieur, Alexis Bouvier."*[69] (The *thélémistes* have the honor of inviting you to a celebration of François Rabelais with the opening of their Abbaye Thélème, 1 place Pigalle, presided over by their venerable Prior, Alexis Bouvier.)

The interior was medieval and high gothic, a style in fashion at the time. In his mocking and censorious style, Gabriel Astruc thus disparaged the fashion of that year 1885:

"Prisonnière de son titre et pour sacrifier à la mode, elle conserve longtemps un aspect moyen-âgeux. Je pense avec effroi à la gothicomanie de cette époque.

Far left: Portrait de Gustave Maroteau.

Left, below: Le ferrement, la chaîne.

Left above: Félix Buhot, *L'Extérieur de la Taverne de Bagne*, etching. Print Room, Bibliothèque Nationale, Paris.

GARGANTUA SUR LES TOURS NOTRE-DAME

TABLEAU DE L. TANZI, GRAVÉ PAR G. LEMOINE.

(Ce tableau se trouve dans la grande salle du rez-de-chaussée de l'Abbaye de Thélème, place Pigalle.)

Tanzi, *Gargantua sur les terrasses de Notre-Dame*, illustration from the *Courrier Français*, May 23, 1886. Musée de Montmartre, Paris. This is one of the paintings which was displayed on the ground floor at the Abbaye. It portrays the proprietor Alexis Bouvier straddling the towers above Notre-Dame. *Rabelais à Meudon, Les joyeux buveurs*, and *La Kermesse* were hung in other rooms. In the Henri Pille room was a painting by Paul Quinsac, *La Bataille du Pichrocole.* On the first floor, the stained-glass windows designed by Henri Pille represented *L'Amour ou François Ier badinant avec des gentes demoiselles* ("Love or François I flirting with some gentle women"). There are no illustrations of these windows.

L'ABBAYE DE THELEME

Aujourd'hui il ne viendrait à l'idée de personne de faire la fête dans une nef ornée de sombres chapiteaux. Le parfum de la gratinée n'est guère compatible avec un décor de sacristie, fut-elle ornée de symboliques gueules de bois. Vers 1885, les décorateurs ne juraient que par l'ogive et la gargouille." [70]

(Prisoner of its name and constrained by the fashion of the day, it retained a medieval appearance for some time. I shudder when I think of the gothic-mania of those days. Nowadays, no one would ever think of partying in a dark-corniced nave. The odors of cooking au gratin are hardly compatible with a church setting, be it embellished with scenes of ribaldry. Decorators around 1885 swore by the ogive and the gargoyle.)

In a short article which appeared in the *Courrier Français* on February 14, 1886, Emile Goudeau furnished a more detailed description of the interior of the Abbaye de Thélème:

Rabelais sort de son cadre pour trinquer avec les Thélémites.   Dessin de Henri Pille.

Henri Pille, *Rabelais sort de son cadre pour trinquer avec les Thélémistes,* illustration from the *Courrier Français,* May 30, 1886. Musée de Montmartre, Paris. Translated, this illustration is titled, "Rabelais leaves his picture frame to drink with the patrons at the Abbaye de Thélème." The front page of the first issue of these chronicles was illustrated by Henri Pille and dedicated to Rabelais as was fitting for the Abbaye. The front page of the second issue represents a painting by Goeunette, *Sur la terrasse du Luxembourg.* The front page of the third issue represents a painting by Uzès, *La Buste de Rabelais,* inspired by Zacharie Astruc.

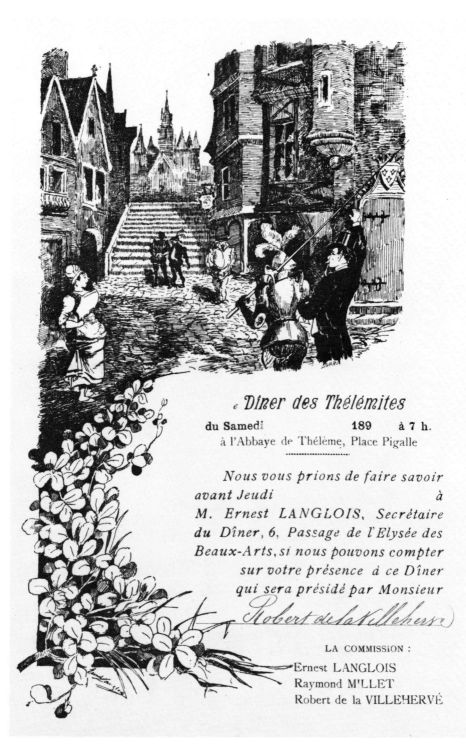

Le dîner des Thélémistes. Musée de Montmartre, Paris.

Dîner des Thélémites

du Samedi   189   à 7 h.
à l'Abbaye de Thélème, Place Pigalle

....

Nous vous prions de faire savoir avant Jeudi   à M. Ernest LANGLOIS, Secrétaire du Dîner, 6, Passage de l'Elysée des Beaux-Arts, si nous pouvons compter sur votre présence à ce Dîner qui sera présidé par Monsieur

Robert de la Villeherve

LA COMMISSION :
Ernest LANGLOIS
Raymond MILLET
Robert de la VILLEHERVÉ

L'ABBAYE DE THÉLÈME

"Voici le premier vestibule d'un style pompeanomoyen-âgeux. Puis un autre vestibule gothique flamboyant, une grande salle Henri II qui s'appelle salle Garnier dans laquelle se trouvent trois panneaux: Rabelais à Meudon, La kermesse, Les joyeux buveurs, *et encore dans une autre salle est accroché:* Gargantua sur les tours Notre-Dame. *Au rez-de-chaussée, encore dans la salle Henri Pille, le plafond est parsemé de chiffres d'or A T, et les fenêtres des baies sont ornées de vitraux d'Henri Pille."*

(The first vestibule—pompous medievalesque style. Then another vestibule in high gothic, a large Henry II room called the Garnier Room decorated with three panels: *Rabelais à Meudon, La kermesse, Les joyeux buveurs,* and in yet another room, *Gargantua sur les tours Notre-Dame.* On the ground floor, again in the Henri Pille Room, the ceiling is strewn with the letters A T inscribed in gold, and the bay windows are embellished with window paintings by Henri Pille.)

To accentuate this medieval atmosphere, the waiters were dressed as monks and the waitresses as nuns.

It appears that the Abbaye de Thélème did not publish its own newspaper. The customers at the Abbaye were mostly journalists from the *Courrier Français,* and for this reason a column entitled *Les Chroniques de l'Abbaye de Thélème* appeared occasionally in the newspaper. [71]

The following announcement appeared in the *Courrier Français* a number of times: *"Messieurs les artistes qui voudraient exposer tableaux, dessins,*

gravures dans la grande salle de l'Abbaye auront droit à un reçu de leurs oeuvres qui ne devront rester exposées que deux mois au plus. . . . " (Gentlemen artists who would like to have their paintings, drawings and etchings exhibited in the main room at the Abbaye will receive receipt for their works. These works will be on display for two months maximum.)

Tanzi, Superelle, Henri Pille and others exhibited their paintings at the Abbaye, but it seems that these shows were neither as consequential nor as successful as those at the Chat Noir.

Henri Pille and Tanzi were the two principle artists to leave their mark on the Abbaye. After 1888, the journalists from the *Courrier Français* tired of the Abbaye de Thélème and preferred the Rat Mort ●

Postcard, the outside of the Abbaye de Thélème. Musée de Montmartre, Paris.

LE MIRLITON

The Mirliton replaced the Chat Noir at 84 boulevard Rochechouart in June 1885. Aristide Bruant, the new proprietor, acquired the lease and the cabaret license through an intermediary so as not to raise the suspicions of Salis.

Aristide Bruant had already made his reputation at the Chat Noir by interpreting his own songs: *A Batignolles, Saint-Ouen, Les P'tits Joyeux, A Saint-Lazare, Aux Bat' d'Af, A Biribi,* and, of course, his famous *Chat Noir,* theme song of Salis's cabaret. But Bruant's behavior, his familiarity, his outspokenness, his coarseness, be it even a certain vulgarity, quickly irritated the customers at the Chat Noir, and they let him know it.

By appropriating Salis's former café, Aristide Bruant was able to take his revenge and, with the Mirliton, become Salis's rival. At the Mirliton, Bruant presided over the evening performances, accompanied by a pianist, the composer P.

Postcard of the façade of the Mirliton. Musée de Montmartre, Paris. When Bruant moved into 84 boulevard Rochechouart, he made no changes in the decor left behind by Salis. The façade remained as it was.

LE MIRLITON

Toulouse-Lautrec, *A Batignolles*, charcoal. Musée Toulouse-Lautrec, Albi.

Toulouse-Lautrec, *Bruant chantant dans son cabaret*, cartoon. Musée Toulouse-Lautrec, Albi. Francis Carco recalls of Bruant: "He sings as he walks or walks as he sings. The clients join in the chorus. When customers come in the café, we shout abuse at them and they are happy. When they leave, we shout abuse at them and they are happy. Last night these very same spectators were at Salis's, who called them, 'My Lords, my Gentlemen, your Highnesses!' and they were happy. Tonight they are at Bruant's who calls them by names of fish, waders or ruminants according to their sex, and they are and still are happy."

Carrière, and by two men he paid to sing the refrains.

The customers at the Mirliton were journalists, artists, boozers and *demi-mondains*. But fashionable society also found it amusing to hang out with the lower class and to be pushed around by the autocratic Bruant who would often greet them with insults and abuse.

Oh! Là, là!
C'tte gueule, c'tte binette
Oh! Là, là!
C'tte gueule qu'il a.

(Oh! Là, Là!
That mug, that yap
Oh! Là, là!
What a mug he has!)

Initiated by Bruant, Friday evenings were reserved for the smart and elegant. Bruant accordingly raised the price of beer on these nights, but even so he always played to a full house.

The atmosphere at the Mirliton was quite different from that at the Chat Noir, less intellectual even though artists and writers such as Steinlen, Anquetin, Bail, Courteline, Métenier and especially Toulouse-Lautrec could be found there. Bruant and Lautrec had always been good friends. In his drawings, Toulouse-Lautrec immortalized the silhouette of Bruant that we know today.

Like other cabarets, the Mirliton had its own newspaper, appearing twice-monthly and later only sporadically. It was published from 1885 to August 1922. Each issue was composed of four pages. There was always an illustration on the cover, either in color or in black and white

LE MIRLITON

Toulouse-Lautrec, *Le refrain de la chaise Louis XIII*, drawing, 1886. Musée Toulouse-Lautrec, Albi. When Salis moved out of 84 boulevard Rochechouart, he forgot a chair. He sent someone to get it, but Bruant refused to hand it over and had it nailed to a wall. All this fuss was the pretext for what became a very popular song:

"Oh! Ladies, what a delight it is

To be seated upon Louis XIII's chair

It belongs to Rodolphe Salis but to Bruant's you must go to sit upon it

"At the Mirli cabaret At the Mirli cabaret

At the Mirliton taine tonton At the Mirliton!"

LE MIRLITON

drawn by Jean Caillou (alias Steinlen), Forain, Uzès, Darré, Durvis, Heindbrinck, Henri Pille and, of course, Toulouse-Lautrec using the pseudonym Tréclau.

In the three other pages of the newspaper, there were poems, stories and, above all, songs written by Bruant. These songs, which were quite popular and familiar to all the customers, were published by Bruant himself in a collection of four volumes entitled *Dans la Rue*. [72]

Thus, Bruant's repertory was glorified at the Mirliton. Anything short of this would have been inconceivable given Bruant's personality.

Worn out by the hectic life as a publican, Bruant sold the cabaret to his pianist, Marius Hervochon, in 1895. Since the atmosphere in the café changed little by little, its fame declined. The cabaret was later renamed the Cabaret Bruant ●

Anonymous, *Aristide Bruant*, photograph. Musée de Montmartre, Paris.

Right: *Intérieur du Mirliton*, illustration from *Plume*, 1891. Musée de Montmartre, Paris. Bruant did not make any changes in the decor left by Salis. All the old bric-a-brac from the first Chat Noir remained as it was in Salis's time.

ARISTIDE BRUANT dans son cabaret du

LE DIVAN JAPONAIS

The Divan Japonais, opened in 1888 at 75 rue des Martyrs, was run by Jehan Sarrazin, an olive merchant with a passion for poetry.

The originality of this café was that *"tout y est chinois"* (everything there is Chinese).

"Dans cette fumisterie de haut goût qu'on a essayé de rendre plus piquante en confiant le service à des dames japonaises encore plus chinoises que le reste—vous retrouverez le matériel du café parisien devenu par un subit changement de décor du japonisme d'occasion. Le billard se peint en bleu et rouge, et on y colle des baguettes de bambou. Au bec de gaz on ajoute des petites clochettes, aux murs on applique des grands panneaux sur soie, comme il s'en trouve dans certains magazines. Le comptoir reçoit également une teinte dans ce bleu et ce rouge qui sont particulières au peuple d'Extrême-Orient." [73]

(In this high-class travesty, whose pungency is heightened by the presence of Japanese serving ladies more Chinese than anything else in the place, you will recognize the Parisian café transformed, by a sudden switch of scenery, into second-hand Japonism. Bamboo chopsticks are glued on red and blue billiard tables. Small bells dangle from gas lights and, as seen in certain magazines, large silk panels hang on the walls. The bar is stained with these same red and blue tints which are particular to the people of the Far East.)

Yvette Guilbert, in her memoirs *La Chanson de Ma Vie*, described the Divan Japonais as:

"Une salle de café de province, basse de plafond et pouvant contenir en les tassant, cent cinquante à deux cents personnes. On y chantait."

(A room in a provincial café with a low ceiling that could pack in a hundred and fifty to two hundred people. Everyone sang there.)

She then described the platform on which she had to perform:

"Une estrade plantée au fond de la salle à 1m,50 du sol, ce qui m'obligeait à faire attention de ne point lever les bras sans besoin absolu, car alors mes mains se cognaient au plafond, ce plafond où la chaleur de la 'rampe' à gaz montait si forte qu'elle nous mettait la tête dans une fournaise suffocante." [74]

(A platform one-and-a-half meters high at the back of the room which made it difficult for me to raise my arms except when absolutely necessary, for then my hands would hit the ceiling, a ceiling where the heat from the gas footlights was so intense our heads were enclosed in a suffocating furnace.)

It was at this café that Yvette Guilbert made her début singing *Les Vierges:* [75]

L'âme candide, et le front pur
Elles vont les yeux vers l'azur
Les Vierges,
Ce sont des abricots pas mûrs,
Elles ont peu d'charmes mais ils sont dur
'Pour sûr'!
Les Vierges!

(With their guileless souls, their foreheads pure
They lift their eyes up to the blue
The Virgins,
They are apricots unripe,
Few but firm are their charms

LE DIVAN JAPONAIS

To be sure
The Virgins!)

All the bohemia from Montmartre would congregate at the Divan Japonais in the evening: Willette, Forain, Steinlen, Desboutin, Léandre; the poets Emile Goudeau, Courteline, Xanrof; even the musician Erik Satie, and the newspaper publishers of the *Figaro*, the *Courrier Français*, the *Gil Blas* and the *Gaulois*. The evenings were spent reciting verses and listening to songs in a congenial atmosphere while Jehan Sarrazin sold olives, *"12 olives pour 5 sous."*

As a proprietor, Jehan Sarrazin was quite different from Bruant or from Salis: he did not insult his public. He loved poetry and insisted that his guests listen to and appreciate poets and singers.

The Divan Japonais also had its own newspaper, first published as the *Lanterne Japonaise* from October 27, 1888 to April 1889 (16 issues). Its publication later

Postcard of the Divan Japonais on the corner of boulevard Rochechouart and rue des Martyrs. Musée de Montmartre, Paris.

Coll-Toc, *Intérieur du Divan Japonais*, illustration from *Raphael et Gambrinus*. Musée de Montmartre, Paris.

continued under the name *Le Divan Japonais*. The illustrations, in Japanese style, were drawn for the most part by George Auriol.

The popularity of the Divan Japonais reached its peak between 1882 and 1892. Jehan Sarrazin then sold the café to Edouard Fournier who subsequently turned it over to Maxime Lisbonne of the Taverne du Bagne.

In 1893, the Divan Japonais was renamed the Concert Lisbonne. But because of the café's unpopularity, Lisbonne quickly sold it to Gaston Habrekorn. The atmosphere in the café then changed again. Although Dranem[76] was welcome there, Habrekorn's staging of sensual poetry, foreshadowing modern strip-tease, was a far cry from the poems and recitations favored by Jehan Sarrazin ●

Poster, *Eléctions Législatives du 27 janvier 1889.* Musée de Montmartre, Paris. Jehan Sarrazin, wanting to copy Salis, also stood as candidate for the legislative elections in 1889. His platform was full of nonsense, as can be seen in this poster.

Right: *Yvette Guilbert,* taken from "*Le Rire,*" June 5, 1904. Musée de Montmartre, Paris. Too poor to buy a suitable dress for the occasion, Yvette Guilbert put on long black gloves for her first appearance on stage. These gloves were to remain a part of her attire throughout her career.

DÉPARTEMENT DE LA SEINE

Élection Législative du 27 janvier 1889

Parisiens et Gens de Banlieue !

Que demandez-vous ?
Qu'on vous fiche la Paix, n'est-ce pas !
Nul mieux que moi ne saurait remplir cet alléchant programme.
Directeur, depuis peu, du **Divan Japonais**, où le Vacarme semblait avoir élu un perpétuel domicile, j'ai su, en moins de rien, faire de cet établissement le dernier asile du Calme et des Bonnes Manières.
Grâce à quoi ?
Vous le savez: Grâce à mes Olives, à mes divines et pacifiantes Olives.
J'ai réussi au **Divan Japonais** ; je triompherai au Parlement.
D'ailleurs, mon programme est bien simple :
Puisque la question de la Constitution divise tout le monde, je supprime la Constitution. On n'aura pas besoin de la reviser. Ça n'est pas plus malin que ça !

Citoyens et Messieurs !

Le 27 janvier prochain, vos bulletins ne porteront qu'un nom, le seul, le vrai, celui qui est sur toutes vos lèvres et dans tous vos cœurs, celui de

Jehan SARRAZIN

LE POÈTE AUX OLIVES

Directeur du **DIVAN JAPONAIS**

Rue des Martyrs, MONTMARTRE.

Vu : le Candidat,
Jehan SARRAZIN.

PARIS. — IMPRIMERIE CHARLES BLOT, RUE BLEUE.

LE RIRE A L'ÉTRANGER

YVETTE GUILBERT

... L'instant suprêm' d' la guillotine;
Alors, un beau jour on m' dira:
« C'est pour c' matin, fait's vot' toilette! »
J' sortirai, la foule salu'ra
Ma tête!
(*Lustige Blätter*, Berlin.)

FOOTNOTES

1. Léon Daudet, *Souvenirs Littéraires, Salons et Journaux* (Paris: Bernard Grasset, 1968), p. 331.

2. Ibid., p. 150.

3. *Journal des Goncourt*, Vol. I (Paris: Fasquerelle et Flammarion, 1956), p. 283.

4. John Grand-Carteret, *Raphael et Gambrinus* (Paris), p. 8.

5. The students felt the need to get together in the evening over dinner.

6. Obviously these are not palettes which artists used for their paint, but palettes on which works of art were painted.

7. During the shadow theatre performance, a "bonimenteur" provided a running commentary to accompany the action, improvising his text and changing its effects according to audience reaction.

8. The Bon Bock dinners date from February 1875 when some poets, musicians and chansonniers decided to get together to "honor" Manet. There were over 400 of these dinners held on the second Tuesday of each month from 1875 to 1905 in different montmartrois restaurants. For each dinner there was a specially designed menu for a different artist.

9. "Etouffer un perroquet" (to smother or choke a parrot) was a nineteenth-century expression which meant to drink absinthe. Absinthe was green like the feathers of a parrot.

10. Edmond Bazire, *Manet* (Paris: A. Quantin, 1884), p. 30.

11. An entry on Manet's *Intérieur de café*, 1869, written by one of Manet's friends (either Henri Guérard or Georges Lucas) states that the café is the Guerbois.

12. Armand Sylvestre, *Au pays des souvenirs* (Paris: Librairie Illustrée, 1892), Ch. XIII, pp. 151-179.

13. Mario Petrone, "La double vie de Louis Seguin de Duranty," in the *Gazette des Beaux-Arts* (Paris: December 1976).

14. Emile Zola, *L'Oeuvre* (Paris: Le livre de poche, 1969), pp. 96-101.

15. Edmond Bazire, *Manet*, p. 32.

16. According to Willette, Petit, a painter of flowers, was a ridiculously small man. Was Petit his name or merely a nickname?

17. George Moore, *Confessions of a Young Englishman*, p. 114.

18. Ibid., p. 113.

19. Georges Paul Collet, *George Moore et la France*, an undated letter addressed to E. A. Boyd, p. 13.

20. Letter from Paul Alexis to Zola (Paris: Bibliothèque Nationale, 1879).

21. *Journal des Goncourt*, Vol. III, p. 245.

22. Daniel Halévy, *Degas parle* (Paris-Geneva: La Palatine, 1953), p. 47.

23. John Rewald, *Histoire de l'Impressionnisme* (Paris: Albin Michel, 1955), pp. 73-79.

24. Manet painted a portrait of his friend Marcellin Desboutin whom he had met at the meetings at the Guerbois. Desboutin, having lived in Venice for a long time, liked to speak Italian, but his accent was very comical. He always took his children along to the café.

25. Manet can be recognized in the description author Grave Imprudence gives of his hero Brissot: "According to witnesses, he, Brissot, such a haughty and caustic person, can be seen for free at the Nouvelle Sparte." Félicien Champsaur also used the Nouvelle Athènes in his novel, *Dinah Samuel*.

26. Stéphane Mallarmé was a great admirer of Manet's work. He wrote articles strongly defending Manet's paintings and on several occasions asked Manet to illustrate his poems.

27. Adolphe Willette, *Feu Pierrot*, p. 108.

28. Roland Manuel, *Maurice Ravel et son oeuvre* (Paris: Durand, 1914).

29. *Journal des Goncourt*, Vol. IV.

30. François Porché, *Verlaine tel qu'il fut* (Paris: Flammarion, 1934), p. 83.

31. Gabriel Astruc, *Pavillon des fantômes*, p. 103.

32. Daniel Halévy, *Degas parle*, p. 26.

33. Candide, "La Nouvelle Athènes," in *La Cité* (Paris, January 18, 1891).

34. Félicien Champsaur, "Le Rat Mort," in the *Revue Moderne et Naturaliste*, p. 345.

35. *Courrier Français* (Paris: October 24, 1896).

36. Panurge is a character from Rabelais's *Pantagruel*, written in 1532. A dissolute rake, drinker and debauchee, Panurge revelled in all of life's pleasures. His most famous adventure was the "sheep" adventure, hence the expression "Panurge's sheep."

37. Adolphe Willette, *Feu Pierrot*, p. 110.

38. Gustave Geffroy, *Claude Monet, sa vie, son temps, son oeuvre* (Paris: Crès, 1922), Vol. 2, p. 10.

FOOTNOTES

39. Daniel Wildenstein, *Manet*, "Bock sur une palette," Vol. I. (Paris: Pierre Collection, 1973). The date does not correspond to the period during which Manet frequented the Grande Pinte. However, it can be assumed that this is indeed the palette Manet painted for Laplace.

40. The Hydropaths, as they were jokingly known, were members of a literary circle that met together in the Latin Quarter during 1878-1879.

41. From 1881 to 1885 the Chat Noir was located at 85 boulevard Rochechouart. In June 1885, Salis moved it to 12 rue de Laval (today, rue Victor Massé).

42. *Journal des Goncourt*, Vol. I, p. 887.

43. Gabriel Astruc, *Pavillon des fantômes*, p. 97.

44. Henri Gervex, *Souvenirs*, pp. 51-87.

45. Ibid., p. 88.

46. The Bibliothèque Nationale in Paris has only six of the seven issues promised by Gabriel Astruc. *Pavillon des fantômes*, p. 101.

47. Léon Gandillot was a gay bohemian and faithful habitué of "La Roche."

48. Paul Gauguin, *Avant et après* (Paris: Crès, 1923) p. 177.

49. John Grand-Carteret, *Raphael et Gambrinus*, p. 156.

50. *Correspondance Générale de Vincent Van Gogh* (Paris: Gallimard-Grasset, 1961), Vol. 8, lettre 510F.

51. There are crayon illustrations of Segatori in a private collection.

52. Toulouse-Lautrec, *Portrait de Van Gogh*, pastel, D. 278 (Stedelijk, Amsterdam). The round table seems to indicate that the Tambourin was the setting for this painting. The Tambourin was one of the only cafés with round tables; the others were rectangular.

53. *Correspondance Générale de Vincent Van Gogh*, Vol. 3, lettres 461, 462 F.

54. *Centenaire du Chat Noir.* Exhibition at the Musée de Montmartre, Paris. May-December 1981. Catalogue by Mariel Oberthür. *Autour du Chat Noir* by Mariel Oberthür in *Connaissance des Arts* (Paris: August 1981).

55. A few of Willette's drawings were published by Léon Vannier in 1884 in a collection entitled *Pauvre Pierrot.*

56. Maurice Donnay, poet-turned-acamedic, long after his appearances at the Chat Noir never forgot the celebrated cabaret where he started out: "I found the right path, at least for the time being. It was not a highway but a pleasant road strewn with flowers. I had never had such good times before. Salis gave me twenty francs an evening to recite Phryné before large audiences who came to see the new show."

57. Salis asked George Auriol to illustrate the first pages of the programs for the Shadow Theatre, the *Chat Noir Journal*, and a few other publications. The style of these illustrations is very Japanese.

58. Paul Thomaschet was born in Trons, Switzerland on the 16th of October, 1839. Like many other publicans in Paris, he came from the canton of Grisons. He ran the Rhin Brasserie, 1 place de la Sorbonne, before he opened the Auberge de Clou. Lautrec did several portraits of Thomaschet.

59. Adolphe Willette, *Feu Pierrot*, p. 169.

60. *Correspondance Générale de Vincent Van Gogh*, Vol. 3.

61. To this day, no trace of these shadow theatre productions, their scenery or their music has been found. These two plays are mentioned by Michel Herbert in *Chansons à Montmartre.*

62. Rodolphe Darzens, *Nuits à Paris*, p. 117.

63. John Grand-Carteret, *Raphael et Gambrinus*, p. 136.

64. These paintings might have been the works of Lautrec, Miguel Utrillo or Picasso. Toulouse-Lautrec did three drawings of the proprietors of the Clou:

Thomaschet et Sescau

Le Père Thomaschet au Café du Clou

Ernesto, Neveu du Père Thomaschet

65. René Dumesnil, *Portraits de Musiciens Français*, p. 106.

FOOTNOTES

66. Maxime Lisbonne opened several cafés and cabarets:

1885—Taverne du Bagne, 2 boulevard de Clichy.

1886—La taverne de la Révolution française, 18 rue de Rambuteau. A tavern where the waiters were dressed as the kings of France.

1888—Brasserie des Frites Révolutionnaires, 54 boulevard de Clichy, where, depending on the way the customer wanted his fries, they would be served by waiters dressed as Napoléon III, Louis-Philippe, or Boulanger.

1889—Lisbonne reopened the Taverne du Bagne.

1893—Aux Politiques, 17 rue du Faubourg Montmartre, Casino des Concierges, 73 rue Pigalle.

1893-1894—Divan Japonais, 75 rue des Martyrs.

1898, January—Jockey Club de Montmartre, 58 rue Notre-Dame-de-Lorette.

1898, March—Cabaret des Contributions Indirectes, 37 rue de la Rochefoucault.

Lisbonne was born in 1838 and died May 25, 1905 in Ferté-Alais. See his biography in the *Dictionnaire Larousse* and the *Revue Universelle* (Paris: Larousse).

67. *Soupe de canaque* was made with rice, onions, potatoes, peas and tomatoes. The *gourganes de Toulon* was a dish made from different varieties of dried beans.

68. John Grand-Carteret, *Raphael et Gambrinus*, p. 148.

69. *Courrier Français*, May 23, 1886.

70. Gabriel Astruc, *Pavillon des fantômes*, p. 102.

71. These chronicles were published in the *Courrier Français* on May 30 and June 6, 1886.

72. A list of Bruant's songs is catalogued in the *Mirliton* of August 1905, number 21 (third series). In the *Mirliton* of August 1906, number 22 (third series), there is an announcement of the release of Bruant's repertory recorded by the artist himself.

73. John Grand-Carteret, *Raphael et Gambrinus*, p. 184.

74. Yvette Guilbert, *La chanson de ma vie*, p. 86.

75. Yvette Guilbert, on the Divan Japonais: "At the Divan, I was overjoyed right away with the public and pleased to sing for them. Sarrazin paid me twenty francs an evening. I therefore made forty francs a day (with the Moulin); for me, still so poor, it was a fortune!"

76. Dranem (1869-1935) was a comic singer who appeared at the Divan Japonais in 1894. His repertory of songs and monologues studded with comical expressions and repetition made the audience laugh as did his costume. He appeared on stage in a chequered suit, trousers too short, jacket too tight, enormous shoes and a tiny little hat on his head.

BIBLIOGRAPHY

Acker, Paul. *Humour et humoristes* (Paris: Simonis Empis, 1899).

Adam, Marcelle. *Les caricatures de Puvis de Chavannes* (Paris: Librairies Ch. Delagrave, 1905).

Appignianesi, Lisa. *The Cabaret* (New York: Universe Books, 1976).

Ariste, Paul. *La vie et le monde du boulevard (1830-1870)*. Preface de Jacques Boulenger. (Paris: Jules Tallendier).

Astruc, Gabriel. *Pavillon des fantômes* (Paris: Grasset, 1929).

Bayard, Jean-Emile. *Montmartre, hier et aujourd'hui* (Paris: Jouve, 1924).

Bercy, Anne de, and Ziwes, Armand. *A Montmartre . . . le soir* (Paris: Grasset, 1951).

Bercy, Léon de. *Montmartre, ses chansons, poètes et chansonniers* (Paris: H. Daragon, 1902).

Bersaucourt, A. de. "Willette et les cabarets de Montmartre" in *l'Opinion* (Paris: February 20, 1926).

Beuve, Paul. *Iconographie de Adolphe Willette de 1861 à 1909* (Paris: Charles Bosse, 1909).

Blunden, Maria, and Blunden, Godfrey. *Journal de l'Impressionnisme* (Geneva: Skira, 1973).

Boisson, Marius. *Les compagnons de la bohème* (Paris: Jules Tallandier, 1929).

Bouillon, Jean Paul. *Symbolisme et art* (Paris: Encyclopédia Universalis, 1973).

Brisson, Adolphe. "Le Pierrot de Montmartre" in *Annales politiques et littéraires* (February 18, 1906).

Carassus, Emilien. *Le snobisme et les lettres françaises* (Paris: Armand Colin, 1966).

Carco, Francis. *La belle époque au temps de Bruant* (Paris: Gallimard, 1954).

Carel, A. *Les brasseries à femmes de Paris* (Paris: ed. Monnier, 1884).

Casteras, Raymond de. *Avant le Chat Noir, les Hydropathes* (Paris: Messein, 1945).

Charpentier, Octave. *A travers Montmartre* (Paris: Editions d'Art du Croquis, 1921).

Cooper, David. "George Moore and Modern Art" in *Horizon* (Paris: February 1945).

Cros, Charles. *Au café, le collier des griffes* (Paris: Stock, 1908).

Darzens, Rodolphe. *Nuits à Paris* (Paris: E. Dentu, 1889).

Donnay, Maurice. *Des souvenirs* (Paris: A. Fayard, 1933).

Donnay, Maurice. *Mes débuts à Paris* (Paris: A. Fayard, 1937).

Duret, Théodore. *Les peintres impressionnistes* (Paris: Floury, 1906).

Duval, Georges. *Le carnaval parisien. Le quartier Pigalle* (Paris: C. Marpon and E. Flammarion, 1884).

Fosca, François. *Histoire des cafés* (Paris: Firmin-Didot, 1935).

Gervex, Henri. *Souvenirs* (Paris: Flammarion, 1924).

Goudeau, Emile. *Dix ans de bohème* (Paris: Librairie Illustrée, 1888).

Goudeau, Emile. *Tableaux de Paris: Paris qui consomme* (Paris: Beraldi, 1893).

Grand Carteret, John. *Raphael et Gambrinus ou l'art dans la brasserie* (Paris: Louis Westhausser, 1886).

Heltey, H. "Les Jemenfoutistes" in *Lutèce* (Paris: January 5, 1884).

Herberg, Janine. "Champ clos des luttes esthétiques du réalisme à l'impressionnisme: les brasseries et les cafés littéraires du XIX siècle" in *Plaisir de France* (Paris: February, 1970).

Herbert, Michel. *Chanson à Montmartre* (Paris: La Table Ronde, 1962).

Huddleston, Sisley. *Paris Salons, Cafés, Studios: Being Social, Artistic and Literary Memories* (Philadelphia and London: J. B. Lippincott, 1928).

Huysmans, J. K. *L'Art moderne. Certains.* (Paris: October 18, 1975).

Huysmans, J. K. *A rebours. Le drageoir aux épices* (Paris: October 18, 1975).

Jeanne, Paul. *Le théâtre d'ombres à Montmartre* (Paris: Editions des presses modernes du Palais-Royal, 1937).

Jourdain, Frantz. *Les décorés, ceux qui ne le sont pas* (Paris: H. Simonis Empis, 1895).

Jourdain, Frantz. *Né en 76* (Paris: Edition du Pavillon).

Jullian, Philippe. *Montmartre* (Paris, Brussels: Elsevier Sequoia, 1977).

Landormy, Paul. *La musique française après Debussy* (Paris: Gallimard, 1943).

Lemaitre, Jules. *Les Contemporains* (Paris: Société française d'imprimerie et de librairie, 1898).

Lepage, Auguste. *Les cafés politiques et littéraires* (Paris: E. Dentu, 1874).

Letheve, Jacques. *Impressionnistes et symbolistes devant la presse* (Paris: Armand Colin, 1959).

Lop, Ferdinand. *Quartier latin et cafés littéraires* (Paris: Imprimerie Mazarine, 1958).

BIBLIOGRAPHY

Loredan, Larchey. "Tavernes à la mode" in *Le Monde Illustré* (Paris: July 10, 1886).

Lorrain, Jean. *Masques et fantômes* (Paris: October 18, 1974).

Maillard, Firmin. *Les dernières bohèmes, Henri Murger et son temps* (Paris: Sartorens, 1874).

Maillard, Léon. *Les menus et les programmes* (Paris: Librairie Artistique G. Boudet, 1898).

Monteil, Edgar. *Les dernières tavernes de la bohème et le temple de l'humanité* (Paris: Sausset, s.d.).

Montorgueil, Georges. *La vie à Montmartre.* (Paris: G. Boudet, 1899).

Moore, George. *Confessions of a Young Man* (London: T. Werner Laurie Clifford, 1904).

Moore, George. *Mémoires d'une vie morte.* Translation of Jean Aubry. (Paris: Bernard Grasset, 1922).

Moore, George. *Reminiscence of Impressionist Painters* (Dublin: Maunsel, 1929).

Morin, Louis. *Montmartre s'en va* (Paris: J. Borderel, 1908).

Morrow, W. C. *Bohemian Paris of Today.* Notes by Eduard Cucuel. (Philadelphia and London: J. B. Lippincott, 1900).

Pillemont, Georges. "Les cafés littéraires" in *La Revue Française* (Paris: January 6, 1929).

Ple, Robert. "Les humoristes parisiens" in *Les Amis de Paris* (Paris: June and July, 1912).

Raynaud, Ernest. "Le symbolisme et les cafés littéraires" in *Mercure de France* (Paris: June 1, 1936).

Rewald, John. *Paul Cézanne, correspondance* (Paris: Bernard Grasset, 1937).

Rewald, John. *Cézanne, sa vie, son oeuvre, son amitié avec Zola* (Paris: Albin Michel, 1939).

Richard, Noel. *A l'aube du symbolisme* (Paris: A. G. Nizet, 1961).

Roberts-Jones, Philippe. *Dictionnaire des principaux caricaturistes et auteurs de dessins humoristiques ayant travaillé en France de 1860 à 1890* (Brussels: Thèse de doctorat, Université Libre de Bruxelles, 1954).

Roberts-Jones, Philippe. "Les Incohérents et leurs expositions" in *La Gazette des Beaux Arts* (Paris: October 1958).

Roberts-Jones, Philippe. *La presse satirique illustrée entre 1860-1890* (Paris: Institut Français de Presse, 1956).

Roberts-Jones, Philippe. *De Daumier à Lautrec: Essai sur l'histoire de la caricature française entre 1860-1890* (Paris: Les Beaux-Arts, 1960).

Romi. *Gros succès et petits fours* (Paris: Ed Serg, 1967).

Rothenstein, John. *Life and Death of Conder* (London: Dent, 1938).

Rothenstein, John. *Men and Memories* (London: Faber and Faber, 1924).

Rude, Maxime. *Tout Paris au café* (Paris: Maurice Dreyfous, 1877).

Sarrazin, Jehan. *Souvenirs de Montmartre et du quartier latin* (Paris: J. Sarrazin, 1895).

Schanne, Alexandre. *Les souvenirs de Schaunard* (Paris: Charpentier, 1886).

Simons, Arthur. *Coulour Studies in Paris* (London: Chapman and Hall, 1918).

Simons, Arthur. *Parisian Nights* (London: C. W. Beaumont, 1926).

Street, Julian. *Where Paris Dines* (New York: Doubleday/Doran, Garden City, New York, 1929).

Vollard, Amboise. *En écoutant Cézanne, Degas, Renoir* (Paris: Bernard Grasset, 1938).

Warnod, André. *Bals, cafés, et cabarets* (Paris: E. Figuerers, 1913).

Willette, Adolphe. *Feu Pierrot* (Paris: Floury, 1929).

Wissant, G. de *Cafés et cabarets d'autrefois* (Paris: Jules Tallandier, 1928).